With
Their
Islands
Around
Them

With Their Islands Around Them

KENNETH BROWER

HOLT, RINEHART AND WINSTON

New York   Chicago   San Francisco

Copyright © 1974 by Kenneth Brower

Published simultaneously in Canada by Holt, Rinehart
and Winston of Canada, Limited.

Library of Congress Cataloging in Publication Data
Brower, Kenneth, date
  With their islands around them.
   1. Wildlife conservation—Pelew Islands. 2. Natu-
ral history—Pelew Islands. 3. Pelew Islands.
I. Title.
QL84.7.P44B76   333.7′2′09965   74-4455
ISBN 0-03-013121-9

Parts of this book were published
in slightly different form in
The Atlantic Monthly.

FIRST EDITION

Designer: Mary M. Ahern
Printed in the United States of America

IN 1971 I was traveling westward through Micronesia, gathering materials for a Friends of the Earth photographic book on the island wilderness of that part of the Pacific, when I came to Palau, the last archipelago in the chain. Robert Owen, the Chief Conservationist of the Trust Territory, sent me through Palau's limestone islands with officer John Kochi as guide. As Kochi guided, he kept an eye open for poachers and finally, toward the end of the day, he spotted a poacher's boat anchored in a cove. He poled in alongside. I held the poacher's gunwale so we would not drift apart while Kochi searched the boat. In the green jungle above the cove I sensed the dark muzzle of the poacher's gun. I felt his eyes watching while, unarmed, we rifled the boat. It was as Kochi handled the poacher's old shirt, frowning angrily, turning it over in his hands, doing everything but sniff it for clues to its owner, that I first began to sniff at Kochi as a possible subject for a story. That was the moment this book began to exist.

Later, back at the biology lab, I became better acquainted with Robert Owen. I saw that this self-exiled American and his native officer were connected historically as well as personally. Kochi was to replace Owen as chief conservationist: the naturalist-bureaucrat would give way to the naturalist-spearman. The two men were past and future.

I saw that the biology lab, the common ground where Owen and Kochi met daily before going about their very different lives, was important to the story. The lab hilltop would be the book's geographical center.

I was not sure I liked the idea of Kochi's becoming a sort of third-world version of Owen. Kochi was a dedicated conservationist, and I was convinced he would do a good job once he adjusted to life behind a desk. His promotion would be good for the islands, then, but would it be right for the man? What was the greater waste: to take a skillful, essentially contented subsistence fisherman and make him into an administrator, or to allow a potential Muir of the Pacific to spend his life in the strong body of a fisherman? I'm still not sure.

This book would be less polemical than so much of my writing had been before, I decided. I would let issues take a rest, and see if I could make character and place carry the story. It was a little comic, I realize, that I was unable to make a cleaner break, that I chose conservationists to write about and not, say, one of Palau's traditional chiefs.

I had at that time, and I still have, the environmentalist's conviction that wildness is likely to be man's salvation. I have a corollary conviction that Kochi's subsistence skills, or something like them, will be the skills needed in our future. With an ear trained by my conservationist father, I had heard the sputterings of technological civilization when I was a small boy, before they were audible to most. My belief in the eventual failure of that civilization is partly an article of faith, I suppose, and not unlike a fundamentalist preacher's son's belief in Armageddon; but mine is supported by more evidence, I like to think. I believed, and still do, that the dumbest thing the Micronesian people could do, at this late stage in the history of the West, would be to Westernize, to "modernize"; for if Micronesians and the rest of us are smart, the old ways, somewhat modified, will shortly become the new.

Part
One

I

AT THE WESTERN END of the Carolines, in Micronesia's sea of small islands, on the very edge of Oceania, lies the Palau archipelago. The Palaus are on the way to nowhere and are seldom visited. They have a large tract of ocean to themselves. They cluster close together, on sunny days an oasis in the blue desert of the Pacific, on stormy days a gray fleet anchored against the stream.

Northernmost of the group is the atoll of Kayangel. The atoll has one inhabited island, two villages, two hundred residents, and two chiefs. South of the sandy circle of the atoll, on a submarine thread of turquoise reef, hangs the main island of Babeldaob, a pear-shaped, tropic-green pendant. Babeldaob is twenty-five miles long, a very big island for this part of the Pacific. Most of its length was formed by an old volcano, eroded now to a gentle slope and overgrown entirely by jungle and savannah; but at the island's southern end rises another formation—a number of steep coral-limestone hills. The hills are fossil reefs that were forced high into the air by earth movements long ago. Like the volcano, they are now completely covered by vegetation. It is hard to find a metaphor for their peculiar shape; they are cusped like the molars of a carnivorous animal, but this does not convey any of their great beauty. Limestone islands are Palau's geological distinction; nowhere else in the world does their odd and beautiful shape occur so plentifully.

From the southern end of the island, the reef-hills step off land into shallow lagoon waters, becoming islets, and they march southward. They proliferate as they go, yet stay shoulder to shoulder, making a tight and formidable maze. In places the islets combine to make sizable islands in their own right. Chains of these islands, minor archipelagoes, connect the big island of Babeldaob and the central islands of Koror, Arakabesang, and Malakal with the southern islands of Peleliu and Angaur.

The natives of Palau are a varied people. Migrations of Pacific races from several points of the compass have met and mixed here. The small dark continent of New Guinea lies five hundred miles to the south, and New Guinea's Melanesian, or Papuan, influence is strong in many Palau Islanders. These men and women are often nearly black, with an African slimness and an African length of limb. In other Palauans the Malaysian influence dominates. These people are smaller, quicker, lighter-skinned. In still other Palauans there is a Polynesian robustness of the sort you see under the "Primo" T-shirts of Hawaiian football players. And there are combinations of all these.

The Palau Islanders were once a warlike people feared by their nearest neighbors. The neighbors lived far away, happily, and for the most part the Palauans of the several islands fought among themselves. Palauans are still very competitive. Much Palauan energy goes into a shrewd and devious practice of politics, and this native love of intrigue is a trait that foreign rulers have been skillful at using to divide the people. Palauans are the best athletes in Micronesia, and they make the toughest fighters. Their relations with foreigners continue to be a little surly.

In the past century the Palauans have been ruled by four different foreign nations. They would like to rule themselves now, but after all the years they are uncertain that they can. They know they are provincial. They are aware of their weakness in the greater world. Japan and the United States fought several fierce battles here, and in the struggle between the powers, the Palauan people were not even pawns. The islands were strategic, but the people did not figure at all. Palauans generally dislike the Americans, who govern them now, as much or more than they disliked the Japanese. Palauans are strangely inarticulate in their resentment, perhaps partly because there has been, as yet, no native revolutionary thinker to give them voice.

A great migration is presently underway in the Pacific, and in Palau, as elsewhere, it is the great fact of island life. Islanders are leaving the outer islands, small villages, and the subsistence life, and are moving into the district centers. Villages are being abandoned to the very young and the very old, and the traditional life is losing its vitality. For Palauans, the district center is Koror Town, on the central island of Koror. The people who move there are caught between two worlds and are uncomfortable. Their intellects tell them that town means progress, but their hearts remain in the old life. The present is a bad time in the history of all Oceanic people. Their future is formless, and it was never that way before.

In Palau there are young men who have stayed behind, living by their skill with spear and net, and young women living by their skill at taro gardening. The people of Koror Town don't know what to make of these primitives, their childhood friends, whether to be ashamed or proud.

The Palaus are not lighthearted islands. Palauan smiles seldom flash; more often they are slow and thoughtful, or wry. The people have things on their minds. There is laughter, of course, and good jokes and good times, but there is also an undercurrent of melancholy. The melancholy may be something new to Pacific islands, or it may be older than Captain Cook, but it does not go well with palms and sand and blue ocean. It is paradoxical and troubling here, in islands that look so much like paradise.

AMONG THE THINGS the Japanese left in Palau were their genes. Japanese soldiers occupied the place for a long time, and their children are everywhere. On each of the inhabited islands, Japanese people look out from dark Oceanic faces. The Palauans have accommodated this alien blood, making it their own, just as they have all the rest. A half-Japanese is in every way Palauan. His first language is Palauan. He is a member of his mother's clan. His aspirations, prejudices, and memories are Palauan. The mixed-blood boy who dives along with his companions into Palauan waters, and comes up with beer bottles encrusted with coral and inscribed with characters he cannot read, may feel a twinge of extra curiosity, but in no larger way is he different.

Today Japanese tourists are returning in small numbers to Palau. The island of Guam to the north is becoming a honeymoon spot for the young

Japanese couples who can afford it, and a few adventurous couples continue on to Palau, landing on a gravel airfield built by their countrymen before they were born. The young Japanese are slender and good-looking, educated and well-to-do, forever smiling broadly. The men have a sort of Italian taste in clothes—neck scarves and short-sleeved safari jackets crisscrossed always by the straps of several cameras. The girls wear minis.

In Palau they meet barefoot half brothers and sisters. No one told them about this, and it's an unsettling discovery.

The moment comes on the airport bus, when the Japanese tourist pays a vaguely familiar-looking native driver; or at the Western Caroline Trading Company, when the light-skinned salesgirl approaches; or up at the biology lab, when the lab's secretary, Sakiei, who is one of those islanders with more Japanese blood than Palauan, looks up from her typewriter. Japanese eyes meet Palauan-Japanese, and there is a charged pause. "So like us, yet not," say the Japanese eyes, and they look away.

Japanese men feel the moment more acutely than do Japanese women. There seems to be an edge of guilt to the male confusion, though there is no good reason there should be. The crime, if it's a crime at all, is of their fathers. The Japanese eyes nervously search the Palauan face, as if for the measure of consanguinity.

An American visitor feels some of the same unease. American men have been here now for twenty-five years and have left children of their own. The strangeness comes in walking down an island path and meeting someone you recognize from high school or somewhere. The sort of greeting you might give a countryman rises, but dies on your tongue, leaving the taste of guilt there before you quite know why. This is not my countryman. Does he blame me, the legitimate son, for our common blood?

The Japanese man, deposed, visiting a territory controlled by his former enemy, seems the more uneasy of the two. For the American visitor, the occupation of Micronesia is current; the lesson in the face recognized on an island path is not yet framed by history and is not so sharp.

For the American *father* of Palauan children, there is an unhappiness as old as empire. The face he recognizes is his own. If he stays long enough in the islands, he watches his unacknowledged sons grow to manhood, and his daughters to womanhood, while he himself grows old.

There is one American colonial officer whose Palauan employees sometimes catch him staring out the window at the boy mowing his lawn. Everyone on the island knows this boy to be his son. The boy's golden color is warmer than the father's, but the backs of their necks are identical. When the colonial officer feels the Palauan eyes on him, he looks away. He pretends to study the far hills of his lovely, troubled island, or to search the sky for tomorrow's weather.

~ 2

ON A GENTLE SUMMIT of the island of Koror, fringed by banana and papaya trees and darkened regularly by the passage of tropical cumulus overhead, there is a spacious, close-cropped circular lawn. At one end of the lawn is an informal botanical garden. The lawn and the garden are manicured and parklike, the only places in the Palau Islands kept in this condition. The residents of the scattered, ramshackle plywood-and-corrugated-metal town below are fond of the hilltop. It is a small civilized clearing in their jungle.

In the middle of the lawn stand several pale-green buildings. They date from two different periods of occupation—Japanese and American—but because each building stands apart, there is no clash of architectures. Nearest the lawn's center is the Palau Museum, which in Japanese times was a weather station. When new, the Japanese station must have been surpassingly ugly. It is windowless on its first floor and has the proportions of a shoe box—a fine example of the power-utility architecture that the Japanese spread in concrete throughout their Pacific. As a museum it is ugly enough still, except for the blueness of the sky and the greenness of the island, and because with the passage of time there has come a tracery of cracks, a suggestion of incipient ruin, that permits some sympathy.

East of the museum is the prettiest building on the hilltop lawn, the *new* weather station, built early in the American occupation. Its ground floor is as grim and institutional as that of the Japanese, but crowning its roof is a white radio-signal-tracking dome, graceful under the tall cumulus clouds that move unceasingly over the island.

West of the weather dome is the longest and largest of the hilltop buildings. This large building stands on a lower step in the lawn and does not dominate the hilltop. It is a hybrid structure, with walls of Japanese concrete and a roof of American metal. The sign out front says Biology Laboratory in big letters. In smaller letters underneath are Entomology, and then, Plant and Animal Quarantine, and finally Conservation.

The Biology Laboratory of the Trust Territory of the Pacific Islands houses, in its two stories, an insectary, a latrine, an apartment for visiting scientists, a biochemical lab, a storeroom, and an office. The office is the busiest spot in the lab—the heart of the place. The metal desks of the three men who work there have been pushed together to make a single big desk at the center of the room. The chair of Robert Owen, the Chief Conservationist for the Trust Territory, faces the chair of Demei Otobed, the Chief Entomologist. These two men might look directly at one another were it not for a mound of papers and monographs between them. Each man has pushed his desk's impedimenta away from him to make working space. This movement is as instinctive to desk workers as a dog's turning on itself to make its bed, so the resulting hill of papers has a natural logic and inevitability to it, like windrows on the beaches of Palau or the mounds of Palau's land crabs. To see one another, Owen and Otobed must lean outward and take the hill in enfilade. The third chair belongs to John Kochi, the conservation officer for the Palau Islands.

Demei Otobed's desk is the neatest of the three. On its surface are a number of glass vials, some marked "Homoptera: determined," some marked "Homoptera: other than scales." There is a tall stack of insect boxes, about the size and shape of cigar boxes, but nicely made of blond wood, with delicate hook latches. The boxes are labeled, in rising order: Okra Pests, Homoptera, Sweet Potato Pests, Hemiptera, Diptera, Hymenoptera, Curcurbit Pests, Coleoptera. There is one *real* cigar box, labeled Manila Blunts 50. This is filled with vials of assorted small insects, apparently the overflow from the wooden boxes. Near the real cigar box, in a slender bottle that once held Alka-Seltzer tablets and is now nearly full of formalin, is a frog. The frog's nose is out of the fluid, its knees are flexed, its legs are not yet dangling.

It looks exactly the way live frogs do when they have just risen to the surface to breathe—still cautious and not quite relaxed. The truth is, of course, that the frog on Otobed's desk is as relaxed as a frog can be. The frog's body is well preserved below the fluid, but above waterline the unprotected tip of its snout has atrophied and turned white. A small exercise of imagination makes this a frog who has slept in the mud through the winter of some ecological catastrophe, and has risen unknowing to the surface, to poke its nose into an incredibly noxious atmosphere. In some other office this might be a large exercise of imagination, but not here, for the three men who share the room are, among themselves, responsible for the integrity of the Palauan ecosystem.

Robert Owen's desk has no bottled insects or amphibians. Owen today has much less time for biological pursuits than in his first years of Trust Territory service. In the old days he wandered all over the Pacific. He is now deskbound, and that does not sit well with him. He gets restless behind his desk and leaves it often. The desk's surface is entirely occupied by in- and out-boxes, all overflowing with papers.

John Kochi's desk has a single in- and out-box, an ashtray, a stained coffee mug. At the head of the desk is a row of books, among them: *An Ecological Glossary, Reptiles and Amphibians, The Great Chain of Life, A Compilation of Federal Laws Relating to Fish and Wildlife Resources.* Kochi reads English laboriously, but in one night he pushed straight through Rachel Carson's *Silent Spring,* fascinated and unable to put the book down, ignoring the protests of his wife. Kochi plans to attend college in the United States, and two of his desk's books mark off the ground he must cover: *How and Why Discoveries,* a science textbook for children published in 1940, and *A Guide to Graduate Study Programs Leading to the Ph.D. Degree.*

Most of the office wall space is occupied by books and periodicals, in shelves labeled: Ichthyology, Marine Biology, Malacology, Entomology, Biology, Miscellaneous. Along one wall runs a workbench with microscopes and rows of beakers and bottled specimens. The largest bottle contains the preserved head of a monkey, a large male macaque. The macaque was a pet that died when Owen was away from the islands. The Palauans who worked at the lab saved the head, bottling it as a present for him. The bottled head makes newcomers to the office uneasy. It is too large for the bottle, and the nose presses against the glass, distorted like a child's against a store window. After a while the monkey's face becomes familiar and it no longer seems grisly.

One shelf above the workbench has been cleared of its bottles to make room for the drawings of Takesi Suzuki, the Palauan-Japanese who works as scientific draftsman for the lab. Suzuki was the lab's handyman until 1968, when Owen recognized his potential as an artist and sent him for training to the Bishop Museum and the Honolulu Academy of Arts. Having begun it, Owen now feels a responsibility to Suzuki's career, and sometimes he peers through Suzuki's dissecting microscope to make sure that the drawing in progress is true to its specimen. Owen is a biologist, not an artist, and he feels foolish peering. All he can do is count the bristles on an insect's leg or check some similar detail. The number of bristles in the drawing, he has found, is always correct. The Suzuki drawings in the lab office are mostly of Palauan insects. They are framed in cotton-padded, windowed boxes intended to display real butterflies.

Stacked here and there in the office are big insect boxes displaying rows of pinned beetles of a big, black species that looks somehow surly, although dead and under glass. The beetles are horned; small coal-black rhinos stampeding on plains of cotton, their motion arrested by the pins.

The few spots on the office walls that are bare of bookshelves, maps, filing cabinets, bottled specimens, and Suzuki's drawings are occupied by storyboards. Storyboards are Palauan narratives in wood. They are something like our comic strips, but are carved in bas-relief, have no partitions between the episodes, and are seldom comic. Some boards are painted brightly in many colors, and some are monochrome, stained brown with shoe polish to look like hardwood. At present the best boards are of the monochrome variety and are made by a murderer whose work is available at Palau's very informal jail to anyone who wants to bargain with him. This murderer was not always the best artist in Palau. There was a rival, whose right arm the murderer cut off below the elbow. The rival has fashioned himself a wooden arm, and continues to carve, but has never returned to his old form, perhaps wisely. Convicts are never far out of circulation in Palau. The Palauan penal theory is that because the convicts are on an island there is no place for them to escape to and no need to watch them too closely. The convicts work on Koror's roadsides with scarlet numbers on their prison T-shirts and machetes in their hands, under the eyes of unarmed guards.

But the most striking storyboard in the lab office is of the multicolored kind. It tells the story of the Killer Crocodile. Like all storyboards, this one is puzzling to a stranger without an explanation.

There are two species of crocodiles in Palau: the seagoing or estuarine crocodile, *Crocodylus porsus*, and the New Guinea crocodile, *C. novaguineae*. Robert Owen believes that a third species, *C. palustris*, the marsh crocodile, or mugger, was introduced by the Japanese. The mugger has not been seen for some time, and Owen suspects that competition from the more aggressive native species proved too rough for it. Of the native crocodiles, *C. porsus* ranges the more widely in the world—throughout the large islands of the southeastern Pacific, from the Philippines through Indonesia, from Australia to the Fijis. For both native species, Palau is the northernmost Oceanic outpost. The Palau Islands are the only group in Micronesia where they occur, though in 1971 a single large crocodile turned up on the island of Ponape, fifteen hundred miles to the east, to the great dismay of the people there. Saltwater crocodiles are sometimes spotted hundreds of miles at sea. According to Palauan lore they hesitate to make such journeys, for at sea they lose legs to sharks. Speculation is that the crocodile killed on Ponape was a traveler from New Guinea, and hopes are that no others get the same idea, for the saltwater species are the most ferocious crocodiles in the world.

But back to the storyboard. One night in 1965, two Palauans were spearfishing in the channel between the small island of Koror and the large island of Babeldaob. One man dove from the bamboo raft into fifteen feet of water, his spear in one hand and his flashlight in the other. He swam downward. His companion watched from the raft as the waterproof light marked the diver's progress. Suddenly the beam began to wave wildly about, then moved off rapidly in a straight line. Twenty yards from the raft a twelve-foot crocodile broke the surface. The diver was motionless in its jaws, unconscious or dead. The crocodile bore the man off into the darkness.

Four hours later, a police boat found the man's remains under a limestone overhang where the crocodile had dragged him. The diver lay in three feet of water. The crocodile had eaten about forty pounds of him. On recovering the body, the district administrator came immediately to Robert

Owen, who was Palau's resident naturalist, and asked if Owen could trap the man-killer. Owen doubted that he could, but he set about it anyway. He constructed a cage of reinforced steel and heavy mesh. Because the dead man's companion had estimated the crocodile at twelve feet, Owen made his cage twelve feet long. He baited the trap with the body of a dog, placed it under the overhang where the victim had been found, and waited. His Palauan informants had told him that crocodiles return to where they have stashed their food. The trap was checked regularly, and after ten days a crocodile was found in it. The reptile was twelve feet, three inches long, almost exactly the estimated size. It had somehow turned around in its own length and was facing the door of the cage. Owen's men pushed two-by-fours through the mesh, pressing the crocodile to the floor and immobilizing it, but not before it had splintered the boards badly. They succeeded in tieing the mouth shut, but Owen's wrist was gashed and his watch torn off afterward anyway by the thrashing of the head. A crocodile's teeth protrude wickedly even when its jaws are closed.

Owen took the crocodile, tightly bound and drugged, to Palau's small hospital and had it X-rayed. It was the first time a crocodile had been X-rayed, so far as Owen knew. The film of the stomach revealed human bones. It was announced that the killer had been captured, and a panic was averted.

Owen wanted to keep the crocodile alive. He thought that a man-killer crocodile, with the X-ray plates to prove it, would be worth several thousand dollars to an American circus. The money would go to the dead man's widow and his twelve children. But the Palauans felt differently. They decided that the crocodile should die, and in the following days Owen's staff confiscated a number of knives from Palauan men intent on its execution. One Palauan did succeed in getting to the immobilized crocodile. It was an old woman, who was discovered jumping up and down on the armored head. Owen did his best, but one day he was called away on business, and when he returned the crocodile was dead—killed, he is certain, by Palauan poison. So the killer crocodile never made the circus circuit. It is now stuffed and on display at the Smithsonian Institution.

Owen shakes his head when he remembers the episode. Killing the crocodile was irrational, he thinks. He has never really understood why the Palauans did it.

The board that tells the crocodile's story was a gift to Owen from the carver. In its first scene, the board shows the diver gracefully leaning to dive from the raft. The next scene shows him seized at the waist by a huge, red-toothed crocodile. The third scene shows the crocodile in Owen's cage, about to seize the bait, and the final scene shows it on the X-ray table. Traditionally storyboard artists symbolize conversation by carving jagged lines, like lightning, from the mouths of their figures. The author of Owen's board has modified that symbol, increasing its amplitude, to make it stand for X-rays. The crocodile lies sorrowfully on the table, being explored by five red X-rays.

BELOW the laboratory hilltop, to the north and west, lies the Pacific Ocean. In the other direction lies a small inland sea called Iwayama Bay. "Rock Mountain Bay," the Japanese named it, for its waters are broken by the steep hummocks of the limestone islands. Koror itself is part volcanic island, part limestone island. From Koror chains of limestone islands stretch away to the south. In the American period they have been called Rock Islands, but it's a poor name. The last thing they look is rocky. The coral limestone of which they are made is entirely covered by jungle, and no rock is visible. The Palauan name for the islands is softer, *elabaob.* The meaning is the same "rock islands," but somehow the Palauan word is more evocative of the shape. The Palauan language evolved on these very islands, and the word was tailored just for them. The shape of the word in the mouth is faithful to the shape of the landform.

The elabaob islands look like somebody's idea of islands. They look, to invent an Oceanic myth, like high islands made by a divine voyager from a low atoll, who had to design them from hearsay, with no models for his hills but the thunderheads that build over the Pacific or the coral heads that build under it. The island forms look fluid. They are flowing in fact. Coral limestone dissolves in water more easily than most rock, and the island summits are melting away under tropical rains at the rapid rate, in a geological sense, of four inches per century. Thus the fossil reefs that were uplifted in the Tertiary to make these islands are in the present returning to their matrix ocean.

At waterline the islands are oddly undercut. Date mussels, sponges, iron-toothed chitons, and several marine microorganisms, all feeding on the limestone between high and low tidelines, have, along with solution erosion, eaten deeply into the rock, circumcising each island and setting each islet on a pedestal. The smaller islets look like very squat and solid toadstools.

The elabaob waters are home for dugongs, crocodiles, green turtles, hawksbill turtles, sea snakes, goatfish, parrotfish, porcupinefish, butterfly fish, rabbitfish, squirrelfish, unicornfish, trumpetfish, surgeonfish, rudderfish, sailfish, snappers, dolphins, wrasses, groupers, sharks, rays, barracuda, moray eels, and countless other swimming creatures. Sea cucumbers, jellyfish, starfish, marine snails, octopi, feather worms, clams, and corals occur in a greater variety and profusion than in any other waters of the world. Marine biologists who have visited the islands estimate that more than half of the marine organisms of Palau's reefs are undescribed and new to science.

The dry land of the islands is home for tree frogs, hermit crabs, centipedes, millipedes, fruit bats, geckoes, boa constrictors, tree snakes, tropic birds, terns, cormorants, herons, ospreys, incubator birds, and parrots. Nowhere in the world, in Robert Owen's opinion, do marine and terrestrial environments of more scientific interest come together. It was this elabaob fecundity that captured Owen and kept him in the Palau Islands.

In the mornings the light on the elabaob hills is soft and the waters of the bay are magical. The sun climbs quickly this near the equator, and by ten in the morning much of the magic is gone, but the aspect of the islands continues to change with the passage of cloud shadows and the movement of the sun. Anyone who leaves the biology lab on some errand, or to go home at the end of the day, is greeted always by a new set of islands.

ROBERT OWEN lives in a Samoan-style bungalow on the hilltop. Every morning he walks the fifty yards of lawn between his front door and the laboratory office. He may pause to watch the light on the elabaob hills, or to follow the flight of a bird, or to consider the lilies of his pond. He may stoop to pick up a gum wrapper dropped by a child. Gum wrappers make him angry. This is the hill that Owen built. He planted the hilltop lawn and the botanical garden that borders it, and he takes a proprietary interest. When Owen gets restless behind his desk, he abandons the office to rake and burn leaves and otherwise to look after his grounds. The Palauans who work for him watch this raking and burning and consider it odd.

Owen's ancestry is a general British mixture, with a large portion of Welsh. His face is deeply lined and dark, more from past burnings than from recent burnings by the sun. He is balding in back, but still has plenty of dark hair in front, and he combs this backward. His eyes are deep set, under black, mad-physicist eyebrows—the kind that won't stop growing by themselves and have to be trimmed. There is a strange fold to his upper eyelids. The line of them runs straight across instead of elliptically. This, and the blueness of his eyes in the weathered face, and his deep, resonant, and sometimes beautiful voice, all have an effect slightly sinister.

Owen is fifty-five. He looks somewhat younger, but like a somewhat younger man who has led a life of dissipation. The impression owes largely to Owen's habit of chain-smoking and to his odd, brittle walk—the result of a back operation—and to hookworm, a harsh sun, accidents in the surf, and all the other hazards of life in the tropics. But it owes also to a certain amount of real dissipation, of which Owen is not ashamed. On Owen's shin there is a tattooed dagger. He was "half-looped" in Guam when the tattoo seemed a good idea. It has since been partly effaced—his wife insisted—but the artist's intent remains clear. In a movie Owen would be the villain.

3

ROBERT OWEN decided early that he would be a biologist. As a boy in Seattle his interest moved from trees to insects to birds to reptiles. He was never sure what sort of biologist he wanted to be, and he has not decided yet. For Owen old flames continue to flicker; he has never been able to discard a field of science once he has studied it. His knowledge, like the inner shell of a nautilus, shows all its former houses.

At the University of Washington there was a professor, Trevor Kinkaid, whose excitement about zoology was electric enough to leap the gap and alter the charges of the students around him, among them Owen's. But Kinkaid was just reinforcement. Owen's course was set before that. If the point of his departure can be fixed exactly, it is probably at the junction of the White and Green rivers, below Mount Rainier in Washington, where his family had a cabin. It was around this cabin, and in trips with his father to other parts of the Cascade range and later to the Olympic peninsula, that Owen made his acquaintance with the natural world. In the springtime in eastern Washington, when the rattlesnakes emerged from their dens, Owen caught them by the hundreds and sold them at sports shows in western Washington. He rowed for hours in Puget Sound, dragging a plankton net behind his boat, then studied his catch under a microscope. In this kind of solitary endeavor his career decided itself.

As a young man Owen was wild. He drank a lot and got in trouble often. It may have been that the wildness balanced Owen's sober and solitary pursuit of science, as outrigger balances canoe, and kept him sailing in trim. Or perhaps the troubled times were troubling him. Owen was young in the Depression. He believed in radical solutions, and his parents did not. In this, as in religion, his views diverged from theirs, and in the moral universe he was on his own. But whatever its cause, the wildness became, like biology, a theme of his life.

Owen once spent three days in jail in Laredo, Texas. He was arrested on the way to Mexico on a bat-hunting expedition. He and a fellow student, a man who has since become one of the top bat men in the world, were headed south to collect Mexican bats. The University of Washington had loaded the two with documents, covered with seals, that permitted them to bring a .410-gauge shotgun into Mexico. Owen is a good shot, and he was along mainly as gunman. For this he dressed entirely in black: black shirt, black pants, black homburg. He carried a skinning knife at his belt and his .410 in the crook of his arm. Today he pretends to find nothing unusual in the uniform. "It was a standard bat-shooter's outfit," he claims. It made him a suspicious character, however, and in a public campground near Laredo he was surrounded by large Texas policemen. They asked for his identification. When he reached for his wallet, the Texans thought he was going for the skinning knife, and three of them jumped him. He served his time and the expedition resumed.

Owen has never outgrown his talent for misadventure. He has settled down considerably, but the bat hunter in the black homburg lives somewhere inside. In August 1971, in New Caledonia, Owen attended a symposium on reefs and conservation. By day he sat at the conference table, behind a placard reading, *Territoire sous Tutelle des Iles du Pacifique*. As Chief Conservationist for the Trust Territory of the Pacific Islands, he spoke on the matters that concern him most in life. By night he hit the bars.

One day's session had ended, and Owen was beginning his evening rounds, in the company of the other delegate from the U.S. Trust Territory, a native of Kusaie Island named Bermin, when he saw a Melanesian walking down the street toward them. The Melanesian carried a guitar. There had been a standing joke among the New Caledonia conferees about the absence of Melanesians from the conference table. There was not even a token

Melanesian. The South Pacific Commission, which was hosting the symposium, was supposed to represent three million Melanesians, and where were they? Now, as big as life, a Melanesian was approaching. The Micronesian delegates embraced the Melanesian. Delighted at finding a genuine Melanesian at last, and a good fellow too, they carried him along with them. Bermin was a good guitar player and so was the Melanesian. They sat on the steps of a hotel and sang. Some Samoan delegates appeared in the windows above and joined in. An Englishman in shorts came down with a whiskey bottle. The last thing Owen remembers was sitting under a tree, singing. He woke the next morning with a terrific black eye. The eye had completely closed. He had no recollection of how it happened, but assumed there had been some sort of unpleasantness. His black eye became a popular mystery. It was not solved until several weeks after Owen returned to Palau by way of Seattle, where he had taken home leave. His friend Bermin had learned the true story from a witness, a man named Dave, and he wrote Owen about it.

"After I left you guys, the genuine Melanesian boy followed suit, so you and Dave were left alone, and not wanting to end the night (I should say morning) abruptly, you two went into the bar and dragged the funny-looking waiter to join you. Having had so many shots of straight whiskey, you fell off the stool like a falling timber, face down, and hit a table."

Owen did not have this explanation at the time of his home leave in Seattle. He couldn't tell his parents he didn't know, so he improvised a story. He had been on a mountain expedition in search of the rare *kagu* bird, he said. He had stumbled.

Owen's two children now live in Washington, near his parents. "I decided I'd better keep the story consistent in the Seattle area," Owen says, "so I told the same thing to my daughter. She just looked at me. 'It could only happen to you, Dad,' she said."

IN 1939, at the end of his sophomore year, Owen took an army flying course. War was imminent and the army needed pilots in a hurry. The course was free, and Owen thought, "Why not?" He learned to fly in a float plane on Lake Union in Seattle.

Three years later Owen was flying low over a blue sea, so very low that from time to time his propellers ticked the waves. The sea was not the

Pacific, the ocean of his maturity, but the Mediterranean. The plane was a B-26 Martin Marauder, and Owen was pilot. The Martin Marauder was a slightly underpowered plane, in Owen's opinion. It was a little slow because it was so heavily armored and armed. ("Flying whores, we called them. No visible means of support.") In addition to its bomb load, it carried twelve .50-caliber machine guns—it now takes Owen a moment to add them up in his memory—but Owen liked its clean lines and thought it was the Air Corps' best-looking bomber.

Owen flew in tight formation with two other Marauders. Each plane was armed with six 500-pound bombs. The mission was skip bombing, an effective but dangerous improvisation in the war against German shipping. The skip bombers of Owen's unit never failed to sink their ships, but each team averaged the loss of one of its three Marauders to each mission. Owen had flown two earlier missions, so as he entered this run, his third and last, he was bucking the odds.

When the Marauder formation came within range, Owen and the other pilots fired their machine guns to disrupt the concentration of the German gunners. The Germans had an improvisation of their own: they fired their larger guns at the sea in the path of the planes. Hitting the resulting water-spouts was like hitting a wall, but Owen's plane did not. At the last moment the bombardier released his bombs, and Owen pulled up to clear the masts. The plane, traveling 250 miles per hour at the moment of release, was so close to the water that the bombs had no time to straighten to perpendicular, and they landed flat, to skip over the surface. A few skipped entirely over the ship, but others struck, as they always had before. Owen passed above the ship in the last instant of its life. His bombs had not yet hit. He was so close he could see the sailors running around. He could see their faces.

The Germans had a three-to-one air superiority when Owen arrived in Africa, and his unit took a beating. After one mission he counted a hundred holes in his Marauder. After others he landed with damaged engines. Once, with one engine gone, somewhere over Sicily, but whether the Allied- or Axis-occupied part he did not know, Owen put down on a field full of bomb craters. He was ten miles inside Allied lines, fortunately, and he was greeted by friendly faces. His Marauder was junked in the forced landing, but the Air Corps found him another.

Most of Owen's war was spent in tents and mud, or in billets with bed-bugs. The billets were brick barracks formerly inhabited by the Foreign Legion. They had a slight edge over the tents, Owen thought. For one sweet period, though, Owen lived in a villa on the beach at Carthage. There was wine and girls. The villa was so near the airfield that Owen and his room-mates, when they weren't flying, could watch the returning flights from their doorstep and count the planes. Owen commuted to the airfield in a Volks-wagen command car he had appropriated.

Owen remembers smoking hashish in a long silver pipe with a single-breasted Arab girl. The breast had been removed as punishment for in-fidelity.

"How was it?" he was asked recently.

"About the same as with a girl with two," Owen answered.

"No, I mean the hashish."

"Oh. It was all right, I guess."

Owen remembers buzzing Bedouin caravans. There was a rumor in the Air Corps that the Bedouins sometimes turned GIs over to the Germans, so Owen and the other pilots buzzed caravans in retaliation. The Bedouin camels bucked, threw their loads, and scattered. It must have taken days to collect them, Owen thinks. The Bedouins lay on their backs in the sand and fired their long, banded rifles at the planes. At least one Bedouin had learned by how many yards to lead a Marauder, swinging his silver-ornamented, eight-foot-long, pieced wooden barrel well ahead of it, for one plane returned with a rifle ball in its fuselage.

But most of all Owen remembers snakes. In those days the North African reptile fauna was not well described, and Owen determined to make the best of his opportunity. He spent all his free time in the desert collecting vipers. His superior officers, afraid that the Arabs would get him, insisted that he go armed and that he be accompanied, and Owen usually obeyed. The collection grew quickly. Owen developed his own faster system for preserving specimens. Instead of making two or three slits along the belly and allowing the 10-percent solution of formaldehyde to soak in, as did most herpetolo-gists, Owen injected living snakes in five or six places with a hypodermic. This left the skin unmutilated. The formaldehyde killed the snakes almost instantly, and they could easily be coiled up in the bottle without their guts falling out. Of the enlisted men assigned to guard Owen, one became interested in the project. The others thought he was nuts.

When Owen finished, his collection was enormous. He carried it to a museum in Sardinia when his squadron moved to that island, and arranged that it be sent from there to New York. Somehow it never went. It was sent to the wrong place, he thinks, or perhaps the museum director decided the collection should stay in Sardinia, a place much poorer in snake specimens than America.

Twenty-seven years and two wars later, standing at the bar of the Royal Palauan Hotel, Owen shakes his head just perceptibly. "They *lost* it," he repeats. The bar Owen stands at is not much of a bar. The "Royal" of the Royal Palauan Hotel is an idea someone imported from Hawaii. Palau has never had kings, and there is nothing regal about the hotel. The bar is dim, but not by design. The native dancers of the murky painting on the wall are difficult to make out. A noisy fan, its blades askew, makes slow revolutions against a bare ceiling. The female bartender affects a bored and sullen style. The gin and tonics she mixes have no taste of tonic—one circumstance that the patrons don't seem to mind. Owen stares ahead of him, wondering where his snakes are. He stares, as if by thinking hard enough, here in the Pacific, decades later, he might somehow trace their Mediterranean wanderings in the bar-mirror glass.

Owen completed forty missions in the North African war. He bombed Rommel's forces in Tunisia from Allied bases in Algeria, then moved to Tunisia to bomb targets in Sicily, and then targets in Salerno, and later in central and northern Italy. He took part in the first raid on Rome. The tension and fear always ended for Owen as he pulled up from his bombing run. His habit then was to turn the plane over to his copilot and sleep through the journey home.

One of Owen's copilots was a man named Kapstein, whom he describes as a nervous type. They flew a mission together over Palermo, where the antiaircraft defenses were strong. It was Kapstein's first combat mission, and he was nervous. As they descended into a black smog of flack they heard the distant explosions, and they braced themselves. Then nearer explosions, then a tremendous explosion that shook the plane. From the corner of his eye Owen saw the blur of an object flying at Kapstein, and he saw Kapstein clutch at his chest. Owen kept his eyes ahead. With the bombsights they used in those days, the pilot had to come in perfectly straight, and Owen did his duty, holding the Marauder steady. When the bombardier released his bombs Owen pulled up and instantly looked over at Kapstein. The copilot's eyes were closed and he was still clutching his chest. As Owen watched, Kapstein opened his eyes. He looked down at his chest and at the hand grasping it. He slowly withdrew the hand, peeling back the fingers one at a time, afraid of what he would see. He and Owen looked. Between his chest and the heel of his hand, Kapstein held a rivet. The concussion of the anti-aircraft shell had jarred it from the windscreen, had shot it against him, and gave him, he discovered later, a terrific purple bruise.

At the war's end Owen peeled his own fingers back, in a figurative way, and found everything intact. He went home to Seattle. If there were any soul bruises, you will not learn about them from Owen. He does not volunteer anything about the war. Few people in Palau know that he flew a bomber in it. Owen is a private man. In Palau he is known more as "Owen" than as "Bob." It is his wife, Hera, who says, "Very few men in my husband's squadron came back." Owen will mention in recalling the first raid on Rome that it was announced in advance by public-relations types, and that the Germans shifted fighter planes from the Russian front, and that there was a massacre, but he speaks of it matter-of-factly, with little apparent bitterness, as a man might talk of the inevitability of taxes. To take him at his word, it's not the old fears or the empty bunks of friends who failed to return that haunt him, but his missing vipers.

Yet in a recent paper on Palau, written fast against a deadline, Owen went back to his African days for a metaphor. The words he chose then may be a clue to what principle Africa represents in his private symbolism, as well as to what Palau represents there.

"When I came to Palau twenty years ago," he wrote, "the coral reefs were practically all healthy, abundant with a tremendous variety of marine life and exploited only for the subsistence needs of the people of Palau. In Palau today, although there are many beautiful coral reefs left, there are some areas that are underwater deserts, with the only life seen being those fish that hurriedly swim by, like an airplane flying over the Sahara Desert."

4

IN THE GENUS *Oryctes*, of the tribe Oryctini, of the family Scarabaeidae, of the suborder Lamellicornia, of the order Coleoptera, there is a beetle named *rhinoceros. Oryctes rhinoceros* L., as the bettle is known to the West, or *mengalius* ("coconut eater"), as it is known in Palau, begins life as a small, clear-white, fine-granulated, hard-shelled egg. The egg hatches into a larva. The larva in its first instar is very small, just a tenth of its eventual length and an even smaller fraction of its eventual weight. At this stage the larva is mostly alimentary canal, for its food is decaying wood, very low in nutrition, and the canal must pass a lot. By its second instar the larva's epicranial suture has become more distinct. The left mandible has formed a tooth near the middle of its inner edge. In the third instar, the larva's head darkens. The mandibles develop more complex molar areas. The dorsum begins to bristle.

Between instars the larva molts. As it rests in preparation for each molt, it becomes semitranslucent. Then its thorax swells, the old exoskeleton splits, a colorless fluid is released, and the larva struggles free. The larva is white when it first emerges. In an hour its head and legs have turned pale pink, and in two hours a pale reddish brown.

The larvae of *O. rhinoceros* are very strong. In research on diseases that might be used against the beetle, experimenters had trouble simply infecting the larvae. "The grubs react violently to any disturbance and persistently try

24

to bite the object that is in contact with their bodies," wrote one researcher. The larvae could chew through hardboards and brass screening. They could give an entomologist a painful bite if he was careless. Oral intubation was impossible without a total anesthesia, and the larvae were not easily anesthetized. Because they were log dwellers, with very low oxygen requirements, it took half an hour of exposure to a carbon dioxide atmosphere to knock them out. They revived quickly on being handled and intubated. Researchers discovered that the best method was to pin a larva down with a patch of quarter-inch mesh, apply heavy pressure to keep the larva from squirming, and inject the disease agent through the mesh. The larva's integument was so tough in the second and third instars that the standard 27-gauge injection needles had to be honed before each experiment.

At the end of its third instar, the larva leaves its log and crawls down into the soil to pupate. The pupa is yellowish brown and rubbery. Most of the adult structures are visible, even the embryonic horn that will grow into the striking feature for which *O. rhinoceros* has its name. It is possible at this stage to determine sex, for the male's horn is longer in relation to its breadth than the female's.

The pupa stridulates. By rotating its abdomen slightly, it causes a friction between abdominal segments, and the noise results. The stridulation is fainter and slower than that of the adult male beetle, but more continuous. There is, as one worker wrote, "a distinct vibration when the pupa is held in the hand." The pupa buzzes like a time bomb.

When the adult emerges from the ground, it is a highly sclerotized black beetle with a hard exoskeleton, sharp spines on its tibiae, and powerful muscles in its legs and thorax. Its compound eyes are covered with a thick, transparent cuticle, through which the multiple facets are discernible beneath. Backward from the base of the horn flanges project, protecting the eyes. In this feature the beetle resembles triceratops more than rhinoceros. The head locks into a groove in the prosternum to keep it from wobbling from side to side when the mandibles are chiseling or when the horn is in use as a lever. The brain is small. The heart is seven-chambered. Metamorphosis has been total, and not even in its nervous and digestive systems does the adult resemble the larva. The beetle is a new animal.

It is hard to sense the strength of the adult by handling it directly, because of the spines on its legs, but by placing a book on the beetle's back, bearing down, and trying to stop its movement across the floor, one gets a good idea. It is difficult to hold the beetle. It just scrapes along, like Atlas. It makes the human pressing down giddy, and he wants to laugh. He feels silly and a little scared.

The male sex organ, the aedeagus, is a large, heavily sclerotized, hooked structure that is entirely retracted within the body when the male is not copulating. In the average male, the aedeagus measures ten millimeters in length, though in a few it is considerably longer. In some individuals it is less, but this is nothing to worry about. The terminal hook of the aedeagus, called the forceps, is a paired structure, smooth, blackish, and hard.

O. rhinoceros, then, is a big, black, heavily hung, tough, pyknic, irritable beetle. A single adult can kill a palm tree.

The beetle prefers coconut palms, but where these are scarce it will live in other palms and in pandanus, sugarcane, and pineapple. In coconut palms the beetle feeds in the crowns. It burrows into the soft heart of palm, where it feeds on juices from the chewed fibers and on the sweet sap that the injured heart sends up into the beetle tunnels. It is in this heart of palm that the tree's embryonic fronds are furled. When a beetle has fed there, the new fronds pushing up from the crown are bilaterally notched, like the snowflakes children cut in folded paper.

Deep within the heart—in the palm's heart of hearts—there is a growing point. It is about the size of an apple, and though it is not likely that this apple tastes better than the rest of the heart, the beetle's mandibles sometimes take him through it, and the tree then dies, for palms, unlike most other trees, have no alternate growing points.

The death of the palm does not end its trials. When the frondless pole of a dead tree has decayed sufficiently, female rhinoceros beetles lay their eggs in the bark of the upper portion. The eggs hatch, and the larvae eat their way downward. The bark remains intact, but after a time encloses nothing but sawdust, larva feces, and larvae. One day the stump blows over in the wind. Cushioned by the sawdust, few larvae are hurt. They resume eating as if nothing had happened. They grow through their remaining instars, then burrow into the soil to pupate. The beetle has, man and boy, erased an entire tree.

26

The reproductive potential of the beetle is crushing. Dr. Linly Gressit, a student of *Oryctes,* estimates that the average female lays 90 eggs in her lifetime. With an average cycle of one month, and assuming a one-to-one sex ratio, she gives rise to a theoretical 186,390 progeny at the end of the first year and 16,995,293,890 at the end of the second, each of which offspring, if its burrowing takes it through the tree's growing point, could kill a coconut palm. If the world had that many coconut palms.

Insects are notorious, of course, for this capacity to multiply on paper. In an insect's native land, there are predators and other mitigating forces that have evolved along with it to keep such numbers only theoretical. The origin of the genus *Oryctes* is Africa, and the homeland of the species *rhinoceros* is Southeast Asia, both of which are places with numerous *Oryctes* predators of all phyla, shapes, and sizes. But in small oceanic islands with the simple ecosystems characteristic of Oceania, places where the genus is unknown, there are no such marshals and deputies waiting to greet the beetle.

Around 1942 the beetle arrived in Palau. It most probably came as a stowaway on a Japanese vessel from Malaya, Indonesia, or the Philippines. The Japanese colonial government was too preoccupied with its Pacific war to eradicate the beetle in the first months, while eradication was still a possibility. Then the war reached Palau itself. In the bombing and shelling, thousands of coconut palms were felled. Logs lay about on every island, making ideal breeding material. The Devil himself could not have designed a more perfect beetle paradise. The beetle population quickly reached critical mass and exploded. Within ten years of introduction, the beetle had killed more than half of Palau's coconut palms. Many of the trees that survived were injured and their copra production was sharply reduced. The damage in Palau was the worst in the world.

So the horned insect's god was Mars, and war brought it to the Palau Islands. The insect in turn brought Robert Owen.

"FROM THE FIRST DAY, I knew it was the place," Owen remembers. "Someone, I can't remember who, took me all through the limestone islands in a small boat. They were so beautiful. So green and full of life."

Owen says little more about it. The decision seems to have been, for him, the wordless sort that a coconut makes when it washes to rest on sand, or an anadromous fish when it feels the opposition of its natal stream. Perhaps for Owen it was the modeling of the limestone islands. Palau's limestone islands are less like real islands than like expositions of the idea of shape. Maybe Owen played that against his still-fresh memory of an airplane over the Sahara Desert.

After leaving the Air Corps, Owen had worked as port entomologist in Hoboken and Seattle before the chance came to work in the Pacific. He jumped at it, and moved with his wife to Guam. In 1949, on loan from the Department of Agriculture, he was conducting a general entomological survey for the navy, which then administered the Trust Territory, when the navy asked him to go to Palau and investigate the beetle.

Owen surveyed the damage and wrote a strong report. The control program begun in 1947 was a failure, he said. Its bounty system, a dollar paid for each dead palm cut down, was ill-conceived. There was no follow-up to assure that the bounty trees were destroyed after they were felled, a failure that could well leave the beetle with more breeding material than before. Nor was there any guarantee that the bounty trees really had been dead. "Certainly," wrote Owen, "the prospect of immediately making a dollar by cutting down a tree must have frequently seemed more expedient to the natives than waiting for the tree to produce a dollar's worth of copra." There was no evidence that *Scolia ruficornis,* the wasp introduced to Palau as a biological control, had become established. Neither was there any certainty that, once established, the wasp would be effective. "Unless an effective sanitary program is pursued or a successful biological control is found," Owen concluded, "the rhinoceros beetle will inflict increasing damage on the coconut trees of the Palau Islands and will eventually spread to Guam and other island groups in the Trust Territory."

This prophecy shook the navy. The prospect of increased damage in Palau was bad enough, but the Palaus are high islands, where other possibilities abound should coconuts fail. In the greater part of Micronesia, in the groups of low atolls, like the Marshalls, where the coconut is the only source of cash and in certain seasons the only source of drinking water (as Owen was careful to point out), the palm is the very tree of life. The beetle's arrival there would be genocidal. The navy asked the Department of Agriculture to look for someone to run a revitalized control program. Agriculture thought immediately of a man.

Robert Owen, asked twenty-three years later whether, in suggesting the new program, *he* had had anyone special in mind, answered, "I had me in mind."

5

THE EFFORT to control the rhinoceros beetle was forty years old in the Pacific when Owen joined it. In September 1909 the bettle had been first observed in Western Samoa. A strict quarantine by the governments of surrounding islands confined it there for many years. Shortly after its Samoan appearance, a biologist named Friederichs began a search of the eastern tropics for a biological control. He found only a green muscardine fungus, which he introduced to Samoa. The fungus had no effect, so Friederichs introduced the European hedgehog and the vole. These were the first of many animals to be pressed into foreign service against the beetle. The hedgehog and the vole, blinking in the Samoan sunshine, were released under the palms. They disappeared into the tropical vegetation, never to be seen again. Accounts of their introduction say simply that they did not survive. They deserve more sympathy. The two rodents were Kipling characters, soldiers who perished in an alien land. They fell on strange soil, without knowing why.

Friederichs next suggested the introduction of two wasps, *Scolia oryctophaga* and *S. carnifax*. *S. oryctophaga* had the right name for the job, certainly. It would eventually take its turn against the beetle, though Friederichs was never able to arrange the introduction himself.

In 1924 the beetle appeared on Wallis Island, four hundred miles north of the British colony of Fiji.

In the 1930s, a British entomologist named Simmonds, then a middle-aged man who had spent much of his career in the Pacific, made an intermittent search of the tropics for a good beetle parasite. In 1935 he searched Malaya without finding anything. In 1939 he traveled to Java, Mauritius, Madagascar, and Zanzibar. He discovered no parasites specific to *O. rhinoceros,* but found that other species of the genus *Oryctes* were held in close check by a number of predators. He set about finding a predator that would work in Samoa. First he shipped a large number of *S. oryctophaga* from Madagascar to Samoa, but the "*Oryctes* eater" failed to establish itself. Simmonds guessed that the reason was the absence in Samoa of Madagascar's cool season. He turned elsewhere. In correspondence with the Zanzibar Museum he learned that *S. carnifax* was an efficient *Oryctes* predator. He tested *S. carnifax* in Mauritius, but was unable to get the wasp interested in the *Oryctes* grubs in his laboratory. When he reached Zanzibar, he discovered that the museum's *S. carnifax* specimen was mislabeled. It was not *S. carnifax,* but *S. ruficornis,* He tested this wasp, and it proved to be the real predator.

S. ruficornis is a big, blue-black wasp with ice-blue wings. Its hind pair of legs are hairy and remarkably long and muscular. It has an abdomen like a bomb, swelling full and ominous, then narrowing sharply to its fatal point. Simmonds considered the wasp promising in that the Zanzibar climate was much like Samoa's, without a cool season, and the wasp would feel at home. The wasp was a gamble, however, in that it was not a true parasite of the coconut rhinoceros beetle, only of the beetle's cousins. Simmonds released the wasp in Samoa, and it established itself. The fact of establishment meant that *S. ruficornis* had made the adjustment to the new species of beetle, for there was nothing else in Samoa for the female wasp to parasitize when she laid her eggs. In time *S. ruficornis* seemed to have some effect in controlling beetle numbers.

There had been no other developments in beetle science at the time Owen began his control work in Palau. Friederichs's search for a solution had begun before Owen's birth; yet in the years following the beetle's 1909 debut, Palau was only the third place in Oceania it had reached, and worry about the insect was still local. The danger to the Pacific was mostly a potential danger. There were few workers and little money available for beetle research.

In 1950, the year Owen began work, an antibeetle course was being taught at the Teachers' Training College in Samoa. The course is a measure of how the beetle was being fought in those days.

"Ask the class how many legs an insect has," the future teachers of Samoa were advised. "Show them a Coconut Beetle and let them count its legs. They will then know that the Coconut Beetle is an insect like a hornet or a cockroach. Show the children the round white egg of the Coconut Beetle. Ask the children what it is. Ask them if they have ever found any eggs like this one."

This sort of thing goes over in Samoa, perhaps, but in Palau it might not. Palauans are suspicious people. In class Palauan children have a formidable reserve and consider it vain and unseemly to be eager with an answer. The teacher now seemed to be asking them to inform on some eggs.

"After about two weeks the egg hatches and out comes the little grub. The grub eats and eats and eats and grows very quickly." Yet this was the little creature the children were supposed to turn over to the authorities. "Ask the children if they can see any eyes on the grub's head. They will not be able to see any eyes because the grub has no eyes." Surely at this point the gentler Samoan students began to worry, vaguely, about their teacher. ("No, teacher, I don't see any eyes. Do *you* see any eyes?")

But the teaching plan had one good suggestion: "Ask the children a few questions about what Samoa would be like without coconut trees."

OWEN STARTED by organizing a sanitation program. Sanitation was then the only effective method of controlling *Oryctes*, and it remains the basic method today. It is costly, hard, unending work. Dead stumps are cut down and hauled to the sea. Vegetable refuse is buried or scattered. By force of human labor, the female beetle is denied a place to lay her eggs.

From the beginning, Owen's campaign against the beetle was a curiously moderated one. "I didn't want to use chain saws and tractors," he says, "because once the people in the villages saw it done that way, they wouldn't want to go back to the simple ways."

It was Owen's professional judgment that the beetle could never be eradicated in Palau, only kept under control. This meant that for the rest of time, or at least until the islands were reclaimed by the sea, Palauans would have to coexist with the beetle. The United States had promised to return the territory it held in trust to the owners, and when that day came, Owen did not want Palauans dependent on a foreign technology. He ordered carabao as draft animals for the log hauling. In December 1950 his first four carabao arrived from Guam. He rode the lead animal up Koror's dirt road, an event that Palauans remember today. They had not seen carabao since Japanese times. All the old Japanese carabao had been eaten during the American siege.

In one of his first quarterly reports Owen wrote that, according to the chief of Melekeiok, the beetle was breeding in the nesting mounds of incubator birds. Owen began a brief life history of the incubator bird, or megapode, describing how it uses its big feet to kick up mounds of soil and fallen vegetation, then lays its eggs within, to be incubated by the heat of the composting material. The megapode's life history becomes a very long aside in Owen's report, and reads almost as if Owen did not realize where his thoughts had taken him. It looks strange in the middle of the report. It may have raised some eyebrows at headquarters.

The chief of Melekeiok's story was likely true. Owen concluded. "If so, it raises a rather delicate problem. The incubator bird is a rare and unique native bird well deserving protection. On the other hand, if it provides sufficient breeding material for Oryctes rhinoceros. . . ?"

Owen may have been a man of divided loyalties, but he worked hard nonetheless. He traveled about Palau, supervising his sanitation crews and learning about the islands. There is a photograph of him from those days. In it Owen walks the beach at Peleliu, along with the *obak*—the chief of Peleliu—and several other dark-skinned residents. He looks much the same now. He walks a little apart from the others, his head down, studying the sand in his path. Beyond the strand, above the heads of the walkers, a forest of dead palms, beetle-killed, stands like a row of burned matches.

IN 1952 the beetle appeared on Vava'u in Tonga. In 1953 it reached Fiji.

Proclamation
By his Excellency Sir Ronald Herbert Garvey, Knight Com-

mander of the Most Distinguished Order of Saint Michael and Saint George, Member of the Most Excellent Order of the British Empire, Governor and Commander-in-Chief in and over the Colony of Fiji.

In exercise of the powers conferred on me by section 10 of the Noxious Weeds and Diseases of Plants Act do hereby declare the area described hereunder to be infected with the insect pest known as the Rhinoceros Beetle.

Viti Levu and all of the islands within five miles of the coast thereof.

Given under my hand and the Public Seal of the Colony at Suva 22nd day of July, 1953.

God Save the Queen

The beetle was now becoming everyone's problem, and Owen wanted a Pacific-wide campaign against it. As a member of the Invertebrate Consultant Committee for the Pacific (ICCP), a committee of the Pacific Science Board of the National Research Council, Owen pushed for international co-operation. The ICCP approached the South Pacific Commission (SPC), an international organization based in New Caledonia, and asked that the SPC become coordinating agency for the various groups fighting the beetle. The SPC had been hearing similar sentiments from other parts of the Pacific, and it agreed to play a coordinating role.

In 1953 the SPC stated the problem. Eradication was not a possibility, the commission said. Workers would have to be satisfied by simply controlling the beetle's numbers. Sanitation was the only sure method of control, but it was costly. Insecticides would not work, for at no time in its life cycle was the beetle sufficiently exposed. As a larva it fed within logs, as a pupa it reposed beneath the soil, and as an adult it fed deep in the palm heart. Palm crowns could be individually treated with a benzene hexachloride mixture with some effect in repelling the adult beetle, but this required a large labor force and more money than the copra economies of the Pacific could ever afford. All these things pointed to a biological control—a predator or a disease that would effectively limit beetle populations. The SPC announced its intention to spend its energies in the search for such a control.

In the three million square miles and the thousands of islands of the U.S. Trust Territory, there were only two entomologists. Netherlands New

Guinea had not even one, and other Pacific territories were similarly lacking. As its first act, the SPC hired an Indian entomologist, T. V. Venkatraman, and sent him searching for beetle parasites and predators. They commissioned another entomologist, a resident of Western Samoa, to study the range of the beetle, and they hired a chemist, who began testing palm extracts in a Queensland laboratory in an effort to find a beetle attractant. The budget for the first year was £10,000.

The SPC formed a Technical Advisory Committee on the Rhinoceros Beetle. Appointed as committee members were government entomologists from the French Institute of Oceania, in New Caledonia; the Department of Agriculture, Fiji; the Division of Agriculture, Hollandia, Netherlands New Guinea; the (Australian) Territory of New Guinea; the Department of Agriculture, Pago Pago, American Samoa; the Entomological Research Station, Nelson, New Zealand; and the staff entomologist for the Trust Territory of the Pacific Islands, Robert Owen.

In May of 1954 the roving entomologist, Venkatraman, made his first quarterly report from southern India. He had discovered that beetle larvae lived in cattle manure heaps. They fed gregariously along the edges of manure pits, usually about six to ten inches beneath the surface. He noted that when manure was stored in concrete pits that also drained cattle urine, no larvae were found. Perhaps that was a clue to something. Then he began a list of possible predators, a list that in the next years would become very long. He reported that fowls, crows, ducks, jackals, dogs, squirrels, field rats, and bandicoots all had been observed to dig out the grubs and eat them.

In August 1954 Venkatraman reported from the coastal groves of coconut palms between Cape Comorin and the Malabar border. He had discovered his first promising predator. It was from the family Elateridae, which includes the click beetles and fire beetles of the tropics. His prospect was "a large, shiny reddish-brown elaterid larva with prominent dark head and well developed mandibles." This elaterid larva had the right kind of face, certainly. "As soon as it comes in contact with an *Oryctes* grub," wrote Venkatraman, "it gets hold of it by means of its powerful mandibles and pierces the body and feeds on the body fluid through the punctures made invariably on the thoracic segments." It sounded like a hell of a larva.

Venkatraman reported that in the laboratory one of his elaterids had consumed eighty *Oryctes* grubs. This specimen might have been just a gym fighter, of course, but eighty wins and no losses was an impressive record, even when compiled under the gaze of a friendly scientist. The elaterid had a single character fault: in laboratory conditions it was cannibalistic.

Yet as Robert Owen, sitting at his desk in Palau, read about the elaterid, he failed to become excited. He knew that reproduction in the family Elateridae was too slow. He never entertained the smallest hope that an elaterid would be the answer.

Venkatraman reported several other possibilities. There was a mole cricket, unfortunately also a cannibal. There was a fly, *Sarcophaga fuscicanda*, but it was too flexible in its preference for victims. Venkatraman recommended forgetting about it. There were several bacterial diseases. The trouble with these was that they had to be injected in individual larvae. Spraying the disease agent on the beetle's breeding media did not work.

In February 1955 Venkatraman reported from Ceylon. He had high hopes for the place, for like the Pacific islands it had little seasonal variation in temperature. He wrote that in the wet zone of Ceylon, coconut logs were the beetle's favorite breeding place, though it also used cattle dung and elephant droppings. Then he noted that "Although little attention is paid to coconut cultivation in Ceylon, the palm grows luxuriantly in the important coconut districts, producing high yields. The rhinoceros beetle is present throughout the island but the incidence of the beetle in general was low in the major coconut area." This plenitude of coconut and absence of beetles occurred "in places where the palms are overcrowded with thick undergrowth of weeds and creepers."

In these observations there was a hint at what later would become an effective method of beetle control. If Venkatraman saw it and played with the idea, he soon discarded it. He was intent on finding a parasite. Owen read Venkatraman's latest observations with interest, for he himself had made complementary observations on the effects of dense undergrowth on beetles, and he was thinking of a way to put them to use.

Venkatraman continued. He attributed the low incidence of *Oryctes* in the wet zone of Ceylon to the predations of his elaterid beetle, to the competition of termites for logs, and to the presence among the Ceylonese palms of giant monitor lizards. In the *very* wet zone—the coastal belt near Galle and Tangalla—the monitor lizard appeared to be the principal predator. Monitor lizards were abundant in the coconut-palm estates because the human inhabitants were Buddhists. Buddhists do not kill lizards, so wherever there were Buddhists there were monitors. It was common to see a dozen monitors working a Buddhist coconut garden at one time. They clawed into fallen logs and climbed dead standing trees, searching for grubs. They received some help, Venkatraman added, from the ruddy mongoose.

Owen considered all these possibilities. In Palau he had no ruddy mongooses, unfortunately, but fortunately he did have monitor lizards. Unfortunately, he had no Buddhists. Still, the Palauan people, though they lacked Buddhist compunctions about killing things, did not go out of their way to kill lizards. A Palauan monitor killed a chicken now and then or stole an egg, but the people had no great animosity toward it. They might as well have been Buddhists.

Unfortunately, that made little difference anyway because of the West Indian toad.

The Japanese had introduced the monitor lizard to Palau to control rats, but had then imported, without much foresight, the toad. Toads are easier for a monitor to catch than rats, so the monitors turned to the toads. Unfortunately for the lizard, there are adrenaline glands in the toad's head. A monitor lizard that mouths a toad goes on a trip, for adrenaline is Mother Nature's Methedrine. A number of monitors had overdosed on toad, and the lizard population was on the decline. In Palau, monitor lizards would not be the answer.

Venkatraman next reported from Burma. His stay there would be cut short, he said, because "the internal conditions of that country are unfavorable," but his list of creatures known to kill the rhinoceros beetle had grown. Among the many were a black carabid beetle, a blue beetle, a reduviid bug from Mysore, various mites, a centipede and a tree lizard from Malabar, a lizard from Mysore, and certain Burmese bats and toads. Venkatraman predicted that somewhere in India, Ceylon, Burma, Thailand, Malaya, Indochina, southern China, Hong Kong, or Formosa; in the Hainan Islands, the Ryukus, the Philippines, or the Indonesian Celebes; in Ceram or Amboina, the right predator was waiting to be discovered.

6

NEAR the biology laboratory, inset in the hilltop lawn, is a hexagonal lily pond. Lilies first came to interest Robert Owen when he was in Southeast Asia, where his work for the Trust Territory had taken him. On returning to Palau he built the pond, stocking it with bulbs from Singapore and Java. Blue lilies blossom there in the daytime, and red lilies at night. Beneath the shelter of the lily pads swim hundreds of tadpoles and mosquito fish.

At a fixed hour each evening, large West Indian toads surface among the lilies and begin a migration from pad to pad toward shore. They pause at the shore, then fan out over the lawn.

At the same hour, on a smaller lawn below the laboratory, the lowest leaves of a trimmed bush stir. The declining sun, by the angle of its rays, has told the toads within that their time has come. On one evening four toads simultaneously made their appearance at the edge of the bush, as if on signal. Almost immediately came a fifth and sixth. Each toad made a single hop and waited to see how the evening would greet him. Then one at a time the entire line made two hops. They paused again. Then three hops. The toads alternated the lead, and the line behind the leader seemed to give spiritual covering fire. Meanwhile, on other fronts, from other shrubs, skirmish lines of toads were advancing onto the lawn. And so it goes every night.

As the toads advance, the tall and slender cumulus that always stands over the elabaob hills turns pink. One evening's cloud is so nearly like the clouds of other evenings, leaning at the same slight angle, with summit blown into the same short banner, that they all seem the same cloud. The cloud returns according to its circuits. It moves forever over the islands.

First swiftlets, then bats, begin to hunt above the hilltop lawn. While twilight lasts, the swiftlets and bats are in the air at the same time. There are then three tiers of defense against the evening's insects, each tier moving at a different speed. Highest are the bats, making their fluttering loops and turns. Next are the swiftlets, faster, skimming the surface of the lawn on the racing edges of their wings. Lowest are the toads, stone-still for long periods, but making their own species of calculation. From time to time a toad darts his tongue or hops to a new post.

The dusk deepens until the sky becomes too dark for the swiftlets, and they depart. The bats drop a little lower to fill the vacuum. The Southern Cross rises and slowly rights itself in the heavens. The air stays warm. On rare nights, heat lightning flashes beyond the rim of elabaob islands. The orange light flares always on the same point of the compass, but with a greater or lesser flash, and a bit to the right or left, so that each illumination discloses the far clouds in a different aspect, as if signaling in code their true nature. It seems odd that one part of the sky should hold so much electricity.

Late in the night the bats leave for their limestone caves, or perhaps they ascend and hunt too high to be seen. They leave the hilltop lawn to the giant toads. The toads in their steady way have lasted everyone out. Near the museum building, where the lawn is lit by a small floodlamp, stationary toads sit here and there, like lonesome cowboys in the light of the moon. They stay perfectly still until a walker is about to step on them, then hop away along their escape routes to the shadowy margins of the lawn.

On clear nights the real moon rises very large on the elabaob horizon. As it climbs a halo begins to shine around it, like a perfect reef encircling an island. At zenith this lunar reef is about twenty thousand miles across. The tall cloud forever marching above the elabaob hills leans luminous in the moonlight.

At 8:15 every night, just as the red lilies are opening in the pond, the metal doors open beneath the bulbous dome of the weather station, and the weather balloon is launched. The balloon fills while anchored to a steel table inside the station door. When its size is right, a Palauan technician shuts off the helium, attaches an instrument box to the tail end of a length of line, and switches on the small light that will mark the balloon's ascent. He takes up the slack of the line, unties the balloon from the table, and walks out into the night. The balloon follows, bobbing above his head. Standing well clear of the station, he opens the hand that took up the slack. The balloon tumbles upward, its shape suddenly elongated as the gas inside tries to rise faster than the rubber that contains it. Then the rubber in its elasticity catches up with the gas and tries to pass. This two-way race heavenward is arrested rudely by the pull of the line, for the technician has kept a grip on the instrument box all the time. It was a false start. The technician waits for several counts, until the balloon is calm and the line is straight up and down above him. Then his hands fall away from the box. The balloon lurches upward again, and its light rises into the blackness.

The entire purpose of the Koror weather station rides with the balloon. The tracking dome exists to keep the balloon's radio signal in fix. The men working beneath the dome note the modulation of the signal and refer to their calibration tables to translate the modulation into information on temperature, humidity, and pressure. The direction the balloon takes tells about prevalent winds. Once a minute, the twelve-dollar instrument box sends down an elevation and azimuth trace. The balloon's high-altitude soundings, correlated with data from similar balloons launched from similar stations scattered across the Pacific, are used for long-range, worldwide forecasting. The Koror station sends up two balloons daily, one in the morning and one at night.

The balloon has an easy ride, usually. The upward temperature gradient is smooth in the tropics. There are no strong counterwinds of the kind that in other latitudes shear the tops off cumulous clouds, broadening them and making them massive. This smoothness is why the nightly elabaob cloud can rise so tall.

After a half hour of steady ascent the balloon is at eighteen thousand feet, where the temperature is below freezing. The climb continues for an hour or more. On an average flight the balloon reaches ninety thousand feet and expands to the size of a four-room house before being burst by its expanding helium. Sometimes at night the balloon fails to make it through the tropopause—the interval between troposphere and stratosphere. The tropopause is the coldest of the zones above the earth, sometimes $-120°$ Fahrenheit, and this cold is deepest, oddly, over the equatorial regions. If it rains at night, with no sun to dry the balloon before such profound temperatures are reached, the rainwater freezes and the balloon explodes.

As the balloon drifts up into higher and colder shells of the earth's atmosphere, the Palauan technicians work below in the electric brightness within the station, wearing short sleeves in the warm Palauan night, receiving with the boredom of routine the balloon's messages. The machines the Palauans monitor are impressive. A chart taped beneath one reads:

6 Hourly Synoptic
(2 cr lf ltr ZCZC (5 sp 2 cr lf)
SMKA PTRO 230000 (ltr 2 cr lf)
SYNOP (2 cr lf)
91408 80512 etc. (ltr 2 cr 8 lf)
3 hourly same except SIKA

Occasionally a shipment of the balloon instrument boxes is delayed, for Palau is not on the way to anyplace, and ships call irregularly. Sometimes the station runs out of its reserve supply of boxes. The balloon is sent up anyway, to be visually tracked simply for information on prevalent winds. A Palauan weatherman checks its progress with a sextant. The sextant's tripod is set on the lawn outside the station door, with legs spread in the grass.

On the daytime flight of one of these instrumentless balloons, the weatherman works under the shade of a brightly colored umbrella, the kind that on the other side of the world would advertise Cinzano, but that here, in a different sphere of influence, advertises Asahi beer. For the nighttime flight, the umbrella is, of course, not necessary. At night the balloon carries just a light at the trailing end of its line. The lurch off the ground sets the pendulum of the light to swinging in a slow arc. As the balloon gains altitude, this movement is minimized by distance. The arc becomes shorter and shorter, harder and harder to detect, until finally it is undetectable, and the light takes its place among the stars.

South of the gibbous weather dome, in the moon shadows cast by the trees that edge the lawn, is the wooden *abai*, or meeting house, where the unfinished watercolors of Carl Gibbons rest for the night. Gibbons is an old Palauan man who remembers another epoch. In Gibbons's youth a pair of watchman gods made nightly rounds among moon and stars, checking on them. The depths of space were not so vast or frigid then. The red rays of the setting sun were projectiles the sun threw to frighten away sharks before it settled into the sea. The navigators of that epoch found their way among the constellations without instruments by a system of dead reckoning. They steered on star courses memorized by the hundreds through long apprenticeships, holding to their course by their feel for the origin of the waves passing under the canoe, letting their intuition measure the drift of the current and the distance traveled on each bearing. The old navigators did not know so precisely as modern navigators where they were, in one sense, but in another sense they knew better. They divided the year into year-east and year-west, naming the seasons for the direction the wind blew. In March, a month in which the wind falls at dusk to pick up again in the morning, the wind spent the night in a certain bush common to the elaboab hills. The wind relieved itself there in the course of the night, giving the bush its bad odor.

It is hard to know how much of this former system the old man Gibbons accepts today. He is aware of the Western bias for theories that are testable, and like most Palauans he likes to give answers that will make an American questioner happy. When speaking in English about the old beliefs, he affects an indulgent smile. But if helium had been an element in the former universe, Gibbons would now have two theories to choose between. The balloon story they tell at the weather station is a good story, but the Palauan story would have been good too, and Gibbons might have preferred it. A Palauan version would begin probably with the escape of the helium from the prison of its metal canister. Then the helium would yearn for outer space—more a mother to the elements than earth is, after all. Then the race homeward. Then the menace of the tropopause, and finally at ninety thousand feet the explosion, not in termination but in triumph.

Gibbons is custodian of the abai, a long, high-peaked, steep-pitched, thatched-roof meeting house built for the Palau Museum in the traditional manner. He works for Hera Owen, who is the museum director. On weekdays Gibbons sits in the abai's cool gallery and paints scenes from his boyhood. There are few visitors and he is seldom interrupted. His watercolors have a Grandma Moses freedom from worry about perspective. His ocean waves and his elabaob ridgelines are stylized, and all his white terns and his noddy terns are painted standing on their tails in the air, but none of these shortcuts seem to save him much time. He works slowly, sometimes pausing and studying the painting for a long time.

The men in his paintings wear the *thu*, the wide loincloth of the Caroline Islands. They wear their hair long, arranged in a sort of bun. They hunt fruit bats and pigeons in Gibbons's jungles with their blowguns, and they dive underwater to spear Gibbons's fish. Dotted lines from the spear-men's hands show the paths their spears have traveled. The men sail, fight, and build. The women in his painting wear amulets on tight necklaces. Their arms are tattooed in black. They cultivate taro, weave, cook. They guide younger sisters through the ritual of first childbirth, and they prepare the dead. The pigs for Gibbons's feasts lie cut up in the prescribed portions, to be distributed according to rank. Sliced taro, arrayed on mats, awaits his feasters, along with bright-colored fish in woven baskets and coconut-flower sap in the tall kegs from which it will be dispensed.

One Gibbons man stands on a platform high in a *bkau* tree. The tree is on Babeldaob Island, and the man is hunting fruit bats. The man may be Gibbons himself, for Gibbons once hunted bats on this very tree. Every September in Palau, bats from Peleliu and the elabaob islands migrate north to a certain part of Babeldaob, and the bkau tree stands on the flyway. The tree's platform is placed in a spot where the avenue through the branches is restricted, and the big bats have little room to dodge about. The hunter in the picture is armed with a net, into which a doomed bat is flying. The net has a long handle, like a butterfly net, so that if the bat swerves the hunter can shift to intercept it. When a bat is in the netting, the hunter will flip the net over so it can't escape. He'll pick the bat out by the tip of its wing, whirl it several times to disorient it, then slam it against the platform, killing it. He'll look quickly upward, ready for the next bat. It was a good method of hunting, Gibbons says. He likes to remember it. The bkau tree was a good spot, he says, a very *good* spot. Trying to explain, he loads the English word with more meaning than it can carry. In season, he says, a hunter returned from the tree weighted down with bats.

Another painting. Under a Gibbons sky of an improbable blue, a group of Gibbons women labor in a field of wetland taro. The field is divided into patches by raised earthen dikes that intersect like wandering paths at the center of the painting. Each of the five patches shows a different stage of taro cultivation. This is not just a device on the artist's part, for in Palau's absence of real seasons such an arrangement of patches, coming to fruition at different times, is possible and desirable. Gibbons brings it off without seeming didactic. One garden lies fallow, black with the promise of fertility. ("The taro garden is the mother of our life," Palauans say.) In a second garden, a group of women prepare the soil. Two of them carry green bundles of compost. Three others, having made knives of their hands, are bending to cut the swampy earth into cubes. When the cubes are lifted out, the compost will be placed in the hole and the cubes replaced on top. The women wear grass skirts and green turbans folded from leaves of giant swamp taro. For the pleasure of companionship they work together, though each taro patch is individually owned. They sing dirty songs as they work. Gibbons has not figured a way to convey the dirty songs in his painting, but such songs are sung in the taro garden and nowhere else. Gibbons knows about the songs only by hearsay. Men must stay away from the taro gardens. The Palauan male's phrase for gossip or mindless chatter is *tekoi el eliuis*, "words of the taro garden," for such is what men imagine the conversation there to be like. But all these are hidden dimensions of Gibbons's painting, apparent only to Palauans.

In a third garden a woman works alone. A basket of taro tubers—her planting stock—rests near her on the dry earth of the dike. Her hands are in the soil, planting tubers.

In a fourth garden, empty of people, the taro is beginning to leaf.

In a fifth garden the taro is full grown. The mature taro is of four varieties, each of which Gibbons has painted a different green. Giant taro, with leaves like the ears of elephants, dominates the other varieties.

Where the dikes meet at the center of the gardens, there is a thatch shelter. The women will come here to rest or to wait out any rain that falls. In midafternoon, in the privacy of the shelter, the women will change clothes. Near the shelter stands an old woman, giving directions and singing magic words to assure a good crop. The magic words are not audible in the painting, but Gibbons hears them.

44

Taro cultivation has not changed much since Gibbons was young, nor has bat hunting. Women no longer wear grass skirts, but they still sing dirty songs among their taro plants. Fruit bats still migrate past the bkau tree, and older Palauan men, wearing khaki shorts now instead of *thus,* still catch them with nets. But other things have changed.

"In my time," Gibbons says, "when I was thirteen, Koror Town was full of pigeons. We could shoot them between the houses. Now you have to go to elabaob to get pigeons." Palauans must travel farther for reef fish, too. "We used to catch many fish right around these mangroves. Now we must go way out to that point for fish."

One of Gibbons's paintings shows a method of fishing no longer practiced in Palau. The painting shows only the harvest of fish, none of the preparation, but Gibbons will explain it to anyone who is interested. First, he says, the people tied the fronds of a native palm, *demailei,* into a great rope three hundred fathoms long. They loaded it into a large canoe and paddled out into the lagoon when the tide was high. They towed the rope into a circle, anchored it, and paddled ashore again. The demailei ring floated untended, its fronds hanging downward like a curtain. At low tide the fishermen returned and stationed themselves around the ring's circumference in waist-deep water. Within the ring swam thousands of fish. No one knew why the fish had remained there. They could easily have swum under the dangling fronds while the tide was high, and they could still swim between the fronds, as the fishermen began beating the water with bamboo, but for some reason they did not. They fled instead to the center of the ring. The fishermen tightened it, continuing to beat the water. When the ring was constricted to nothing, and there was no room inside for the fish, they swam into nets at the canoe rather than brave the palm fronds. Gibbons does not know why the fish were leery of the fronds. The improbability of the method tickles him.

"You don't catch any rabbitfish that way," he adds. Rabbitfish swam through the fronds without a second thought, probably because their habitat was eelgrass, and the green bars of the demailei prison looked like home to them. The good sense of the rabbitfish pleases Gibbons.

The demailei ring was used only at times of big feasts, Gibbons says, for it produced a ton or two of fish. Gibbons believes the method would still work today. There are enough fish for it, certainly; if there is a problem, he thinks, it is that Palauans no longer practice the kind of community effort required, and they might have trouble organizing.

Recently Gibbons saw a snapshot of his demailei painting. The original had been on exhibition in Hawaii for several months. Gibbons and an old friend spent fifteen minutes passing the snapshot back and forth, chuckling as they studied it. They were seeing more than just Gibbons's handiwork, clearly; they were remembering.

After careful thought about it, Gibbons has decided that the old life was better. Food was more plentiful then, he says. Life was not so busy. The people hunted and fished. They were not so worried about money.

Life then was guided by a concept called *kerreomel*. It was a good concept, Gibbons believes. He smiles when he thinks of it. For Gibbons it is one of those propositions with a satisfying internal logic. Kerreomel meant wise use of things—land, wildlife, food, equipment—so that they would last. Palauans practiced kerreomel privately by saving food and money for a rainy day, and publicly in a number of laws designed to conserve resources. Land use was regulated by authorities in the village and clan. Certain islands were designated as preserves for one wild species or another. In the elabaob islands, for example, it was forbidden to hunt incubator birds. In every municipality there was a man, the "messenger" for the chief, who determined when the pigeon season should open and announced the date. He traveled about the municipality telling the people to have their blowguns ready. The messengers had titles. The messenger for Ibedul—the chief who in the nineteenth century became paramount in Palau and who, like Caesar, gave rise to a succession of ibeduls—was called Rerebai. There was a succession of rerebais. The messenger for Palau's second most powerful chief, the Reklai, had the title Remerang. The men of the lineages that hold these titles have lost their powers, but John Kochi, whose job is to arrest pigeon poachers and the men who use dynamite or Clorox to kill fish, is working in their tradition, and Gibbons approves of his efforts.

Kerreomel was a concept necessary to island civilization. Islanders seem to sense their limits more easily than do continental peoples and to understand more readily that resources are finite. In Palau this understanding became law. It was a *good* law, and older Palauans smile the same odd

46

smile in remembering it. Few Palauans under twenty have heard of ker-reomel. They ask you to please repeat the word.

Gibbons, who is seventy-six years old, has lived to see several epochs pass in Palau. At the conclusion of each epoch, the islands have been a little poorer. The past century has been devolutionary. The Spanish, Germans, Japanese, and Americans have all had their turn at ruling Palau. (Gibbons was named Karl as a boy in German mission school, and now under the Americans he is spelled Carl.) The American epoch, almost everyone in Palau agrees, is the least golden of Palau's ages. None of the Palauan arts is extinct yet, save perhaps tattooing, but under the Americans all arts are doing poorly.

Among the traditions the past century has diminished is the Palauan pharmacopoeia. In 1896, Carl Gibbons's father, William Gibbons, recorded some of the folk remedies in use in his day. William Gibbons was literate, having been taught writing by his own father, James Gibbons, a West Indian who jumped ship in Palau. Carl remembers his father as a meticulous man who recorded everything in a journal. If the sun was shining when William woke in the morning, he noted it. He was a favorite informant of the German ethnographers who came to Palau. Among the remedies that caught William's attention were Lepal of Ngetkib's Cure for an Earache, Sabu's Medicine To Stop Heavy Bleeding, and numerous others.

Lepal of Ngetkib's Cure for an Earache.
Take two tiny, new leaves of the *kollil,* two root ends of the *moulal,* one root of the *lap,* and two of the very new leaves hidden in the heart of a *ti* plant of the *didmechi* variety. Combine the ingredients, grind them up, and place the mixture in a coconut-fiber sheath. Squeeze it through the sheath into a *kikoi* shell or a similar container. Add coconut milk, mix well, and pour the solution into the ear. If the eardrum is broken—as happens sometimes when a diver goes too deep—half of this mixture should be squeezed into the ear, as before. The other half should be mixed with coconut meat that has been grated, fried, and kneaded with water, and this combination should be swallowed. A simpler remedy for sore ears, but nearly as effective, is to warm coconut oil to approximately the temperature of well water heated by the sun, then pour into the ear.

Sabu's Medicine To Stop Heavy Bleeding.

Grind the young, new leaves of *Averrhoa bilimbi* and of *apeokl* in a mortar made from the shell of a giant clam. Place the mixture in a coconut sheath. Dip in seawater, then squeeze slowly over the wound. This medicine speeds healing, as well as stops the flow of blood.

In his journal William Gibbons noted the existence of a small tree, the leaves of which when crushed in the hand, held to the nose, and breathed of deeply, cure headaches. He noted that the juice of three small hot peppers, squeezed through a coconut sheath onto a wound, acts as an anesthetic, and that the *leaves* of the pepper plant, cooked in fresh water, are good for a stingray wound. For a puncture wound, William's sources recommended tearing the flesh open a little and squeezing lime juice into it. This would effect the release of the poisonous fluids.

There were disreputable doctors in Palau, as everywhere. Here and there in William's account are remedies by practitioners who seem to have been quacks. "Yechad of Putalpai's Method for Burning Out a Swelling or an Ache," for example, sounds drastic and doubtful. "Yechad's System for Massaging the Insides of the Body" is intriguing, until you get into it. This Yechad system was simply a medicine that worked internally, Yechad claimed, after it was swallowed. "Yechad's Cure for a Person Who Falls from a Very High Place and Completely Loses His Speech (Although He Can Open His Mouth)" is clearly a fraud—isn't it? But one Yechad cure sounds like a fine idea, especially for a healthy person. The cure must be undertaken in the early morning. Chewing on a special leaf, the patient dives into a freshwater spring or river, and under the surface he washes the leaf down with a drink of the cold water he is swimming in.

ALL THIS healing knowledge, good and bad, is passing or has passed.

The ruins of former greatness are everywhere in Palau.

Palau's oldest meeting house stands in Airai Municipality of Babeldaob Island, on a rise overlooking an *étoile* of cobbled paths. No one knows how old the building is. John Kochi, for whom Airai is home, guesses its age at several hundred years. The walls are an Etruscan red, faded from a stronger color that is no longer manufactured in Palau. The roofline dips deeply at center—plastic and accommodating, like a landform.

Below the meeting house, at the center of the juncture of stone paths, in the spot where Western architects would place a fountain, sits a circular plug of stone. John Kochi calls this the "resting conjunction." The people met here, sat, and talked. Outward from the resting conjunction the cobbled paths radiate, disappearing into the surrounding green forest. Down the middle of each path, the pavement has been worn smooth and shiny by generations of bare feet—a path within a path. The paths are not good for hurrying: the stones are of irregular height, and a walker must watch his step. On either side of each path are stone platforms where houses once stood. The house platforms are widely spaced, for then, as now, Palauans did not like to be crowded. Some platforms still support houses, but many do not, for there are fewer people in Palau today. The islands once supported fifty thousand people, by some estimates, but today, after foreign diseases and wars, there are just fourteen thousand Palauans. The past bustled more, and Palau has fallen from that. The empty platforms are solid, having resisted the roots and seedlings that love to turn stones aside. The platforms are simply rectangles of bare gray stone, and inset in each is the white, scalloped shell of a giant clam. The shells are used as foot basins. They have endured, as chimneys do in the charred ruins of Western houses. Callers once washed their feet in the basins before entering the vanished houses. Today when callers wash their feet, they use buckets, for Palau has fallen, too, from her former grace.

On Koror Island, in the grass behind the museum abai, beneath the windowsill where Carl Gibbons, the custodian, sits and paints his past, there is a small square pavement of stones. At each corner of the square sits a backrest, a smooth monolith about three feet high. The laboratory hilltop was once meeting place for the four chiefs of Koror, and each chief owned a backrest. The square was made small, so that the backrests would sit close together and the chiefs could converse without being overheard. Carl Gibbons himself is ruler, fourth chief of Koror, and one of the backrests belongs to him. The last time Gibbons remembers sitting there was in Japanese times.

Today the stone backrests still lean together conspiratorially, or perhaps just earnestly; yet for more than a quarter of a century they have been mute.

CARL GIBBONS has lived through almost all of Micronesia's recorded history. Today he is like one of those riverbanks whose exposed strata tell the entire story of a plain.

When Gibbons was a boy he traveled to Ponape Island with a German expeditionary force sent to put down a rebellion. He went as an interpreter. There were seven ships, Gibbons remembers, and 570 soldiers from Rabaul and New Guinea. Rebellions like the one in Ponape have been rare in Micronesia. What the Micronesians seem to have lacked more than anything is a leader. Tribal differences kept the people divided. Had there been a hero to rally behind in the beginning, the people might have thrown their rulers out, but later the foreigners were too strong, and today Micronesians have only martyrs. When Micronesians did rebel, their insurrections were sad and hopeless from the beginning, like the wars fought in America by the Indian nations toward the end of the nineteenth century. The Micronesian rebellions required the same bleak courage. Native accounts of those rebellions are remarkably similar in language, and in their undercurrent of resignation, to Indian accounts of their wars. Carl Gibbons has dictated such an account.

"The uprising started because there was a German project—building road—and the person who was in charge of the work gang was a bad man. He was very strict and beats the Ponapeans. So the work gang got together and say, let's figure a way, because we are suffering very much from this beating. So they decided to kill him.

"There is a mangrove channel that separates the island of Sokehs from the main Ponape islands. When the Catholic priest heard about it—about the conspiracy—he wrote a letter to the government and sent a Yapese boy with the letter to warn the Germans. The Sokehs people learned about this, and they got canoes and caught the boy in the Sokehs channel. They threatened the boy and he surrendered the letter. They told him to return or else they will kill him. The priest sent another messenger and the same thing happened. Then the priest told the women to take their laundries and pretend they were going to the stream to wash, and he put the letter in one of the women's hair. The Ponapeans stopped them and searched the laundries but could not find the note. So as soon as the women were out of sight, one of them took the note and ran and gave it to the German administrator. When he read the note he was puzzled because, as he says, the Ponapeans were his 'children' and the people of Sokehs knew him very well."

The administrator decided to investigate, Gibbons says. The administrator's anxious staff warned him to go accompanied by soldiers, but he assured them it was not necessary; when the Sokehs people saw him coming, he said, they would know that their "older brother" had arrived.

The German surveyor who had beaten the work gang was then in hiding in the Sokehs mission, protected for the moment by a group of Ponapean women who sat outside, begging for his life. When the surveyor saw the administrator's skiff approach, he came to the door. The administrator disembarked and had taken three steps from his skiff, when the leader of the conspiracy, a man called Samuel, stepped from behind the church and shot him dead. Then Samuel turned and killed the surveyor.

For seven months afterward, as Gibbons remembers it, the Sokehs rebels fought the Germans. They held out in the island's caves and jungles, where they withstood the barrages of the German warships. The naval guns leveled all the vegetation on a good part of the island, exposing the white rock beneath. (Forty years would pass before Gibbons saw such naked rock again—on Peleliu Island, back home in Palau, after perhaps the bloodiest of all the fighting in the war between America and Japan.) At the end of the seventh month, the German commander decided to find a better approach. "He was afraid," says Gibbons, "that if they kill a lot of people there may be some who knew something about the cause of the uprising, who would die before they told it to the Germans." So the Germans ceased firing. They climbed all the breadfruit trees, knocked down the fruit, and cut it into small pieces so that it would rot quickly. "And when that happened," Gibbons says, "it speeded up the whole fighting. After five days, the first of the natives arrived. This man was a member of the conspiracy. We were gathered at the veranda of the house when the man approach. He was wearing ragged hibiscus-fiber thu. He entered the gate and walked straight to the house."

Gibbons heard the conspirator greet the German commander in the Ponapean language, "*Kaselelia main.*" They shook hands. Through an interpreter, the German asked the man where he came from.

"There is now a new situation in the woods," the man replied. "There isn't any more foods and there is no reason for us to starve in the woods. This thing that we have done was in front of us, it was not from the back. So there is no need for me to hide myself. I came and maybe this afternoon and in the days following they will all be coming in."

And so it was, says Gibbons. "The people kept coming in and coming in, until no one was left in the woods anymore."

A hearing was held, at which the Germans determined that twelve men were responsible and decreed that they would be shot. Among them was Samuel, the leader.

"They then prepared good foods for them and they were also invited to dine with the German administrators, because they were facing the death sentence." An invitation went out to all the people of Ponape. There was a huge feast, and everyone showed up. Afterward the young Gibbons was among those who escorted the doomed men to their mass grave. The rebels were tied with hands behind their backs to stakes above the ditch. As the German soldiers readied themselves to shoot, their officer raised his hand and halted the proceedings. He turned to his Ponapean audience. "Most of you are women," he said. "All of you, if you have male babies, tell them to remember this, and not do as Samuel did." Then the officer ordered his men to resume.

"There were three conspirators who suddenly fainted before the German gave the order to shoot. As soon as the officer in charge said 'Leg on,' these three men toppled over, before they even had bullets in them. When the shots were fired they were all like mosquito nets. It was a very gory and nauseating sight. Every one of the men slumped over except Samuel, who kept standing up, shaking his head. So four soldiers again opened fire, aiming right at his chest, so he finally fell over."

Perhaps it was this man, Samuel, refusing to die, standing and shaking his head, who could have led the Micronesian people to freedom. But his person was required, not just his example. His story might give a Micronesian youth a fine, tragic emotion, but not the kind of emotion that would make him eager to go fight the Germans.

In 1916, the year Robert Owen was born, a Palauan of high clan named Temedad, an acquaintance of Gibbons, suffered a seizure. On reviving, Temedad announced that he had made contact with Ngiromokuul, the god of his village. Visions of this sort were common enough among Palauan priests, but in the course of Temedad's, Ngiromokuul delivered an uncommon message. The god had granted him special powers, Temedad claimed, among them control of taboos over certain foods. Temedad immediately lifted the Palauan taboo on bananas, announcing that they were safe to eat. When the fruit was eaten without ill effects, the people considered it miraculous. Shortly afterward, Temedad brought a dead woman to life, and his reputation spread.

This was the beginning of the religion *Modekgnie*. It was an angry religion, in part a reaction to the years of foreign rule. Temedad taught that the world was out of balance and that the foreigners, first the Germans and now the Japanese, were responsible. The phosphate mining on Angaur and the bauxite mining on Babeldaob were a disembowelment of the earth. Lumbering of Palauan forests in disregard of old land-use laws, and fishing that ignored the old fishing rights, had scattered the Palauan gods. The former unity of people, land, and gods had been broken. Modekgnie means "to bring them together." Temedad intended to do that, to restore the unity.

In German times Temedad had been a constable. In 1914, when the Japanese assumed control of Palau, the prophet enrolled in a Japanese carpentry course in Koror Town. Enrolling with him were three other constables from German times, Ongesii, Wasii, and Rngull, all of whom became his disciples in Modekgnie. The direction of the religion would change as each of these men came to control it.

Temedad taught that the Palauan way was best. He pointed out the irrationality of German and Japanese ideas about work. Singing and dancing were obviously better than working overtime in bauxite mines. The subsistence life was the good life. People who farmed and fished and gathered fruit in the forest could not be hurt by the fluctuations of distant markets. There was no need to learn the Japanese language. The Palauan language was good enough.

In 1919 Temedad was betrayed by Palauan Judases and jailed by the Japanese. Rngull took over, and Modekgnie became more businesslike. Rngull was an organizer. He made a lot of money for the religion before he was jailed in 1921 for extortion. Then Temedad was released from jail, and for a time the movement regained its old purpose, but in 1924 the prophet was jailed a second time and he died behind bars. Ongesii assumed control and guided Modekgnie for the next twelve years. Ongesii was a natural bureaucrat who placed functionaries in every Palauan village and built Modekgnie hospitals. By 1937, through Ongesii's work, all the district chiefs and most other title holders in Palau had converted. The chiefs had most to gain from Modekgnie's conservatism, for it protected their titles. The *sons* of chiefs resisted it most strongly, for in Palau's matrilineal society they grew up tasting power, but inherited none of it. They had most to gain from a new order.

The war worked in favor of Modekgnie. The insanity of the foreigners' ways was never more apparent. They were blowing each other up. The Japanese announcement that the Americans were demons invading from Mars drove many Palauans to seek the protection of Modekgnie magic. By 1945, Modekgnie controlled all Palau. Modekgnie remains strong today, especially in those remote villages where the pace of life is measured and sane and where the people seem happiest.

Today in Modekgnie there seems to be more emphasis on magic and less on the preservation of Palauan tradition than there was before. The belief in the subsistence life does not seem so pure. Recently John Kochi had an argument with the present leader of Modekgnie, a man called Big George, when Big George complained that the laws against hunting pigeons and dugongs were un-Palauan. Pigeons and dugongs were traditional Palauan foods, said George, and hunting should not be forbidden. Fine, answered Kochi, so long as you use traditional Palauan weapons. Big George, who almost certainly had never shot a pigeon with a blowgun, did not like Kochi's proposal. But the flavor of Modekgnie has changed before, and someday revisionists like Big George may be replaced by men more in Temedad's mold, men who do not pick and choose what they like in technology, who see instead that the subsistence life is a whole ethic and that therein lies salvation, or revolution.

Perhaps Temedad was the leader Palauans have been waiting for. There are, it's true, some seedy aspects to the history of his religion that might seem to work against him. His disciple Ongesii is said to have magically protected all female converts from venereal disease by having intercourse with them, and Temedad himself raised revenues, they say, by calling in Palauan bead-money for purification and keeping the pieces he liked. Carl Gibbons, who knew Temedad, is skeptical about him. "He found a good business," says Gibbons. "In the Bible he sees a picture of Moses with the stick. He reads about Jesus curing people, so he tries it himself." The prophet's death in jail was a sordid end, certainly. But Calvary is sordid too, without a lot of explanation. Perhaps time will make Temedad's story sweeter.

"Palau will always be for Palauans," Temedad taught. "The Palauan people should never adopt the foreigner's religion and life. We are black and our gods are black. The foreigner is white and his gods are white, so their gods and our gods can never come together."

It was to Temedad's country that Robert Owen, a young entomologist, a white man with white gods, came to do battle with an insect. It was here that Owen chose to make his home.

BY MORNING on the laboratory hilltop the toads have returned to the safety of the lily pond. The night's insects have departed. Carl Gibbons pedals his bicycle past the toads' sentinel posts on the lawn. At the Palau Museum abai he dismounts and sets his kickstand. He enters and resumes work on his paintings. At 8:15 the morning weather balloon rises, and at 8:30 Robert Owen steps outside his bungalow. He pauses to follow the distant flight of a bird. His idea of the superman is one who can identify every plant and animal he sees from his doorstep. This morning Owen satisfies himself as to the species by noting the characteristics of its flight. He continues on to his office.

For a time no one passes. A rainstorm suddenly darkens the hilltop. The sun will soon break out just as suddenly, but for now rain gently falls. Two Palauan girls cross the wet lawn on their way to school. Their black hair is tied in ponytails. They walk slowly, ignoring the rainfall. One girl holds a small guitar under her dress to protect it. As she walks she sings, and underneath her dampening dress she plays her morning music.

7

OWEN'S BEETLE campaign was not far along when he lost his carabao handler. The handler was Jesus C. Maguadog, a Chamorro who had come from Guam with his carabao and his wife. He was an able man and a hard worker, and Owen had made him foreman of the beetle-control crew. Then Maguadog's wife died.

"Maguadog believed she was killed by Palauan medicine—magic," Owen says. "He thought it was A———, an employee of mine at the lab, who had worked the magic. His wife went into a slow decline, for no apparent medical reason. She got weaker and weaker and in a month or so she died. It was a classic case. I went around with Maguadog and we got countermagic. But she died anyway. It starts out as love magic, you know. A———wanted the girl. He put the thing—the magic, the charm—under her mattress or someplace. The way love magic works, if the girl doesn't succumb to you, she begins to get sick and wastes away. So this is what happened to Maguadog's wife. But it's something I don't know much about."

A bitter Jesus Maguadog left the Palaus and returned to Guam. Owen was without a foreman.

Then, in August 1954, as roving entomologist Venkatraman was working his way toward the Malabar border, there was a second crisis in Palau. On the island of Peleliu, where the rhinoceros beetle had destroyed all the coconut palms, Owen had begun a new planting of seven thousand seedlings.

Of these new seedlings, six were attacked by the beetle. In a letter to the high commissioner of the Trust Territory, Owen admitted that six sick seedlings did not sound like much of a crisis, but he assured the high commissioner that it was. He had picked Peleliu for replanting, he explained, in hopes that a success there, on an island hard hit by the beetle, would encourage the Palauans of other islands to replant too. He had been careful to delay the replanting until his sanitation crew had brought Peleliu's beetle numbers down to a safe level. This had *not* been done in 1949, when, on the advice of agriculturalists with no training in entomology, the Peleliu people began a plantation of four thousand seedlings. Of these, all but a hundred were dead, killed by the beetle. If the present planting ended in a failure, Owen wrote, it would mean the end of native participation in the beetle program.

Owen suspected that lying about somewhere was an unknown source of breeding material. Somehow it had been overlooked in the sanitation work. The amount was considerable, or it was very favorably located from the beetle's point of view. With the departure of Maguadog, there was no one whom Owen trusted, besides himself, to find the breeding medium. He was sure he could do it, however. "I have yet to see beetle-damaged coconut trees for which I cannot find the breeding source," he wrote the high commissioner. He requested permission to postpone a scheduled tour of the other districts of the Trust Territory, and the high commissioner consented.

The mounds of Peleliu's incubator birds fell immediately under suspicion. Owen dug into one mound, and from the first thirty shovelfuls of compost he sifted eight mature beetle larvae. It was a disheartening find. Robert Owen is a man who, with a scotch or two under his belt, will confess that his heroes are Audubon and Muir; yet in this matter he could not be like either man. Fifteen more coconut seedlings had been discovered dead. If the incubator mounds proved to be the breeding source, Owen would have to destroy the mounds, and the birds themselves, so that more mounds would not be constructed. His single consolation was that the birds would survive on other Palauan islands where copra was not gathered.

There was another possible breeding medium, however. Sea grass grew abundantly in the shallow water near Peleliu, drifting ashore in windrows that were sometimes two feet high. Once Owen had thought this sea grass would make good compost for coconut palms, assuming that it would be too saline for beetle larvae and therefore safe. To test his assumption he had built two experimental compost heaps near a coconut grove. After three months he broke the heaps open to find a thousand beetle larvae in various stages and more eggs than he could count. The compost idea had ended abruptly. Now Owen wondered whether the sea grass in natural concentrations might be breeding beetles. Perhaps a storm had carried a quantity of it high on some beach, leaving it in a hidden place where the sanitation crew had missed it. The sun and rain might have leached it of salt, and the female beetles might have found it suitable. He sent his sanitation crews to look for such a place. Fortunately, both for the incubator bird and for Owen's peace of mind, they discovered it. The sea grass was destroyed, and the Peleliu plantation was saved.

A year later Owen turned the sanitation program over to the Agriculture Department of the Trust Territory. He devoted his energies to the search for a biological control and to other duties as staff entomologist, but he continued to advise on sanitation matters. His word had weight, for by now he was an old hand in the Trust Territory. The turnover of government employees was rapid, and Owen had six years of service. He was the Father of Beetle Control in his adopted country. When, five months after Owen relinquished control, the agriculturalist in charge of sanitation operations on Peleliu reported that he was routinely destroying the peculiar mounds made by "some species of bird," Owen quickly set the man straight before too much damage was done.

FROM TIME to time in the long campaign against the beetle, rumors of a new bug would come to Palau. A scientist searching a foreign field would stumble upon what looked like *the* bug—the beetle's nemesis. He would describe its laboratory record against the beetle. In subsequent reports he would tout his insect. There were many such bugs, the white hopes of the entomology game.

The white hope with the most advocates was probably *Platymeris rhadamanthus*, a large red-and-black assassin bug. The assassin bug had a pleasantly oryctophagous look. Its biting mouthparts were wickedly curved.

It did not resemble the praying mantis exactly, but it had the mantis animus, the intelligent and lethal head. In the fourth and fifth instars, assassin nymphs attacked and killed beetle larvae; but better than that, the adult assassin bugs killed adult beetles in palm crowns. It was the first predator known to do so. The assassin tipped the beetle on its side, held its prey still with two front legs, and inserted its stylet into the gular region, or between the abdomen and thorax, or ventrally where the head joins the prothorax. In one palm crown under observation by scientists, an assassin bug seized a beetle, slipped its stylet in neatly, "and afterward left the carcass of the beetle hanging by a leg which had become entangled in the fibers." It was a good sordid death for *O. rhinoceros*.

When there was water the assassin bug drank readily, and the frequency of its kills increased. The females were the killers. Occasionally a male would try in a bumbling way to attack a beetle, but he usually failed to dispatch it. One laboratory female assassinated a beetle while she copulated, and afterward she and her mate ate her victim. *P. rhadamanthus* was that kind of girl.

The assassin bug was shipped in all stages of metamorphosis to Fiji, New Guinea, New Caledonia, and Palau. Over a period of several years Owen released thousands of them, usually ten to each palm crown. He was never able to recover any. It was a mystery. The assassin was one of the few predators that Owen had much hope for. They were so easy to raise in the laboratory. There were no disease problems. But they did not take hold in Palau or anywhere else in the Pacific. Owen has no theory why.

There were other white hopes. They kept coming out of the woodwork or out of the jungle. There were white hopes with promising names, like *Neochryopus savagei*, a hardy bug that survived shipment well, and others, like *Scarites dubiosus,* with more doubtful names but good reputations. (*S. dubiosus* was from Assam, a jet-black, voracious feeder that bit first- or second-instar beetle larvae in the head, briskly sucked the contents, and in forty minutes drained the grub dry.) Yet in each of these insects there was a flaw.

Because Africa was the center of dispersion for the genus *Oryctes*, many workers directed their hopes to that continent. An entomologist named Hoyt went searching there. In Sierra Leone, Hoyt seeded several oil-palm logs with *Oryctes* larvae and waited to see what would happen. One log was soon entered by a small grayish rat, which ate several grubs and departed. For two weeks nothing else happened. Then one day all the logs were entered by swarms of driver ants, and all the larvae were eaten. The ants entered through old holes made by xylocopid bees. They ate everything but the head capsules of the larvae. As the entomologists of various Pacific territories read Hoyt's report of this, they imagined, for a moment at least, armies of driver ants marching over their islands. They quickly dismissed the idea, as Hoyt himself dismissed it. "Because of the driver ant's habits," wrote Hoyt, "such an introduction would not be popular with the inhabitants, to say the least."

One autumn an entomologist named Fred Bianchi left Belém, Brazil, and journeyed eight hundred miles up the Amazonas to Manaus. He was looking for predators on the subfamily Dynastinae, which comprises a number of beetle genera in the family Scarabaeidae, of which *O. rhinoceros* is also a member. He hoped to find a predator on Dynastinae that could acquire a taste for *O. rhinoceros*, the distant cousin of its traditional South American victims. (The dynastid beetles are themselves horned and are also called rhinoceros beetles. To avoid confusion, the Pacific beetle is properly called the coconut or Indian rhinoceros beetle.) In South America, where Bianchi now searched, there is a dynastid named the Hercules beetle. It is nearly the largest insect in the world. Males of the species grow more than five inches long and have *two* horns. The predator that could slay this insect Hercules would be promising indeed. Natural law required that some Brazilian creature had devised a way to do it, and Bianchi hoped to find that creature.

Fifteen to twenty dynastid species were said to live in the area, but Bianchi failed to find a single beetle. Brazil was poor country for beetles, he reported, because of the competition for breeding logs from "termites and ants, which crowd the regions to a degree not imaginable by anyone who has not been there." But Bianchi did glimpse one tantalizing possibility.

"I saw on one occasion a very large black scolid wasp," he wrote, "which from its size I judged to be a parasite of some dynastid." Bianchi chased the wasp, but was unable to catch it.

He reported his glimpse of wasp from Panama, where his search for a predator took him next. He wrote by the fitful light of a kerosene lantern, in pencil, in a student's exercise book. The South Pacific Commission received his report, typed and mimeographed it, and sent it out. It arrived at desks in Melanesia and Micronesia, where entomologists glimpsed the wasp in their imaginations. Who *was* the mystery wasp? What species? Had it been the answer? Entomologists throughout the Pacific wondered.

Of all the insect contenders, only *Scolia ruficornis*, the wasp introduced to Samoa by H. W. Simmonds decades before, was at all effective in the Pacific. One by one, the other fair-haired bugs failed. The coconut beetle was still champion. Outside the class Insecta, the list of possible predators continued to grow, but to no avail. Added were the Zanzibar pouched rat, the Zanzibar lemur, scolopendrid centipedes, tree shrews, flying lemurs. In Africa, Hoyt discovered a nematode that was transmitted between beetles during copulation. He tested it. (The entomologists would have stopped at nothing to win.) Unfortunately, it proved impossible to culture the nematodes, and the venereal infection had no dramatic effect on the beetle, anyway.

"Flying lemurs!" dreamed the entomologists as they tossed in bed at night.

The most elusive of the white hopes, and to many workers the most promising, were invisible. Their chief advocate was a man named Surany, an insect pathologist hired by the SPC to investigate beetle diseases. Dr. Surany was certain that microorganisms were the answer. The most promising diseases were what he called the "histolytic" and the "blue" diseases. The histolytic disease was marked, Surany reported, by "widespread or complete disappearance of the adipose tissue as well as histolysis of the muscle and other tissues to various degrees. The moribund or dead larva will become translucent, flaccid, and dehydrates rapidly (in 24–48 hours). Yellowish, clear, sometimes viscous liquid fills out the hemocoel, a derivate of the hemolymph, including, in part of the cases, the hemocytes. The muscles are usually in a relaxed stage and the muscle fibers often disintegrate by breaking up first into myofibrils. The disintegration extends to the apophyses which always separate from the body wall. The integument is reduced to the epicuticle and will become transparent."

It sounded like hell for the larvae. It was enough to evoke sympathy for them, almost, until Surany's conclusion: he noted that the agent causing the disease had not been identified. The pathogen might be a virus, but he did not know for sure. Perhaps an electron microscope would tell. And whatever the pathogen was, it was difficult to transmit to the larvae.

Writing of the blue disease, Surany reported that "moribund larvae are flaccid, and of a faint slate-blue colour turning dark-blue rapidly. They will become black within 24 hours. Characteristic odour resembling fresh mushrooms accompanies the disease." Again, it sounded like an awful thing to wish on anybody, but again the pathogen remained a mystery. The two diseases continued to be called "histolytic" and "blue," after their symptoms, for symptoms were all that was known about them.

Surany kept refining his disease prose. He was a genius at this kind of writing. It was a morbid talent, but it is hard, of course, for a pathologist to be anything else. Elaborating on his description of histolytic disease, Surany wrote: "By the time the larva has reached the moribund stage, the outline of the intestine, with its opaque contents, is easily discernible against the light. The body becomes flaccid and no muscle tonus can be felt. Faint peristalsis of the rectal sack might continue for a while after the pulsation of the heart has stopped. The death point is marked by the cessation of the faint reflexes of the appendages and palpi. . . ."

This must have made cheering reading in Fiji, Tonga, and New Britain in the lean years when the beetle frustrated all attempts at biological control. Perhaps beetle workers kept it handy and read it as Sonny Liston, after losing his title, is rumored to have watched, over and over again, the films of his victories over Patterson.

Dr. Surany was convinced that microorganisms were the principal check on the beetle in its native ecosystems. He felt that the great part of beetle research and money should go to the study of disease. Robert Owen, who read Surany's findings with interest and was happy to see Surany pursuing his line of investigation, was not convinced. One of Owen's strengths was that he never became the advocate of a single method of control. He was certain that when control was achieved, it would be through a combination of methods. This is an old tenet of insect control, and not original with Owen, but many seemed to forget it. Searching for an answer, it was as natural for a pathologist to think disease as for an entomologist to think bug. Owen resisted the temptation. He was one of the least excitable of the beetle workers. His belief from the beginning was that years of work lay ahead and that the problem would never quite be resolved. If some super-insect had emerged from the jungles of Brazil or Africa, and suddenly had driven a terrorized rhinoceros beetle from the Pacific, Owen would have been happy, perhaps, but disillusioned.

In his own research, Owen developed a way to harvest and ship cocoons of *S. ruficornis*. Before this, the wasp had been shipped as an adult, with very high mortality. Owen's cocoons were tough, easily shipped over long distances and long periods of time. This success might have made him an advocate of the scolid wasp, but it did not. He was careful in his claims for the wasp. He reported simply that in Palau, as in Samoa, the wasp *seemed* to have some effect in controlling the beetle.

He was similarly cautious in his claims for vegetative barriers.

The idea of vegetative barriers was Owen's own. He does not remember when it came to him. It was a simple idea, but it did not jump full-blown into his head. He had walked under palm trees for eight years before it became perfectly clear. In his wanderings Owen noticed that beetles were sometimes deflected by a single leaf or twig. "Have you ever seen one of those things fly?" he asks today. "He lifts those armor-plated wing covers, revs up his wings, gets them buzzing, and then staggers off. If he hits a leaf or anything, he folds up and falls to the ground. He has to start again."

Getting airborne again was hard for the beetle. It was seldom able to take off directly from the ground. It had to climb partway up a trunk and then drop off, like a pterodactyl from its cliff. If it encountered an obstacle more than a few times it became exhausted. Owen assumed that this was why beetle damage seemed to be diminished in poorly managed palm plantations where vines and other vegetation grew uninhibited. On a trip to Samoa, Owen had visited both European-style plantations, kept neat and parklike by grazing cattle, and Samoan-style plantations, which were badly managed, according to conventional theory, and he had been struck by how much less the jungly Samoan plantations suffered from the beetle. Apparently the beetles were intercepted before they reached the Samoan palm crowns. Owen began to wonder about deliberately planting such barrier vegetation as a cultural method of beetle control. Would a continuous canopy of trees, a secondary canopy beneath the palm crowns, stop the beetle?

64

Owen's perceptions were an ecologist's. If he had been intent on something less than the whole environment of the beetle, it is doubtful that the barrier idea would have come to him. ("When I came to Micronesia I learned the plants before the insects," he says. "What would be the use of the other way?") He was not watching simply as an entomologist when he saw deflected beetles fold their wings and drop to the ground. For forty years entomologists had seen that, but none had thought to put the observation to use; or if the barrier idea had occurred to them, it did not hold the appeal it held for the man whose heroes were Audubon and Muir. For someone convinced of nature's rightness, the barrier theory was wonderfully gratifying. It rewarded all the principles of the ecologist's faith. If the theory proved true, it meant that palm forests left to themselves were better off. It meant that in diversity is stability. If the forest was allowed to retain some of its original complexity, that complexity would serve as a reservoir of potential from which a new arrival like the rhinoceros beetle, as alien to the place as a creature from another planet, could be held in balance. It meant that the conventional wisdom on coconut palms—that plantations should be monocultures kept carefully bushed and neat—was wrong. What the copra experts were learning in agriculture school was good only in an ideal world where no beetles flew. The real world was uglier than that. There was a horned insect loose in it that cut the hearts from living palms. By simplifying the ecosystem, the monoculturalists were preparing a table for the beetle. They were clearing lofty galleries through which the beetle could sail unimpeded.

Earlier in the beetle campaign, a number of workers had become concerned that the mystique of biological control was diverting too much energy from other possibilities, like light traps and chemical attractants. They were afraid that the idea of finding an insect ally to defeat an insect enemy was too pleasing in a poetic way. But that mystique had nothing on the potential mystique of Owen's barrier idea. A barrier solution did not require any searching of foreign lands. The answer lay right at hand, in natural processes that needed only to be recognized. It was cheaper. If the barrier was natural and the plantation was just left to itself, it would save the entire cost of cultivation. If the barrier was an artificial canopy, of leguminous trees, say, planted to fix nitrogen in soil that coconut palms deplete of nitrogen, then maintenance would still be far less expensive than keeping the plantation bushed.

But Owen kept calm. He set about devising ways to test the idea and to find which kinds of barriers would be most effective. The barrier idea was his own minor *Origin of Species*. (Owen's seems a simple theory, but so does Darwin's, once it has been explained.) He might have been forgiven for pushing it, but he kept it to himself until he was sure.

~ 8

IN 1959 the South Pacific Commission held its first beetle conference at Suva, Fiji. In the welcoming address, which was reprinted in the *Fiji Times* under the head, "Rhinoceros Beetle Battle Is Crucial," the governor's deputy acknowledged Robert Owen's attendance last.

"Finally, we are deeply grateful to the authorities in the United States Trust Territories, and particularly to Mr. Owen, the Staff Entomologist at Palau, who have rendered such valuable assistance by providing us with the first potential rhinoceros beetle parasite, the Scolid wasp, by furnishing us with Scolid cocoons."

For Owen, this Suva conference, at which he would make public his vegetative-barrier theories, was the high point of the beetle campaign. At Suva scientists gathered from all parts of the Pacific, and Owen met the men with whom he had been corresponding for the past decade. Face to face at last, they talked and argued over the conference table at the Grand Pacific Hotel. When the formal sessions ended they adjourned to the hotel's comfortable chairs. Indian waiters brought them whiskey and water, without ice, for the British did not believe in it. And the Indian waiters brought coffee. The hotel bar closed early, and the beetle men adjourned again, this time to Suva's private clubs. Native Fijians were not permitted to drink in those days, and these clubs were the only places still open. (It was a very different Pacific, then; the old-style British colonialism was still in operation. Owen has not been particularly sad to see it pass, but it made things pleasant and comfortable, he says, if your complexion was right.)

The conferees at Suva were without exception impressive men, with vigorous intellects. The conversation was heady for Owen, who as Palau's only biologist had been isolated from men like himself. Among the Suva participants were the grand old men of Pacific entomology. H. W. Simmonds was there, eighty years old, introduced to the conference as the Nestor of the beetle wars. Simmonds had spent a lifetime in the Pacific, with numerous successes against the insects of many islands. Somewhere surely there is a Maugham story about him—the young entomologist traveling by freighter between Apia and some other sunbeaten place. Maugham will have added a terrible secret or a strange twist of fate, but otherwise Simmonds should be recognizable. He was a man of another era. When he and Owen walked together through Fiji's coconut groves, he dressed nattily and carried a walking cane. He did not really need the cane, but it was part of the uniform he always wore in his field work. American colonial officers didn't have his kind of style, and Owen enjoyed it. Owen believed that Simmonds was mule-headed on *Scolia ruficornis*, the wasp the old man had introduced to Samoa more than twenty years before. Simmonds was more hopeful about the wasp than Owen was, but Simmonds would listen to counterarguments. "I loved the old guy," Owen says of him.

Another great old Pacific entomologist, Pemberton of Hawaii, was there. Dr. Pemberton was one of the reasons Hawaiian agriculture was among the most efficient in the world. Hawaii was the only place where sugarcane was grown commercially without the use of insecticides, largely because Pemberton had found other methods of control. Gordon Dunn, a veteran economic entomologist from New Britain, was present too, as was Charles Hoyt, the young entomologist from American Samoa and, lately, Africa.

Others of the beetle fighters at Suva were not scientists, but they were all smart, and Owen learned from them. Alexander Kroon, a Dutchman who had worked in Java until the Indonesians threw the Dutch out, was one of these. He was a rugged man, articulate in English and knowledgeable about beetles. He was the economic development officer for the SPC, and as such he had no biological training, but he had the mind and the energy to venture successfully into the new field. It was Kroon who had organized the conference. A German-Samoan named Muller, the pest-control officer of Tonga, a man then in his seventies, was present. Muller had a high-school education at most, but he was a good observer with a lot of empirical knowledge about beetles. He was the only man in the world who had ever succeeded in eradicating the rhinoceros beetle. His success, on Keppel Island of Tonga, came partly because that island is so small, only six square miles, partly because Tonga is a monarchy and the king had given him all the forced labor he needed, but partly too because of the force of his personality. He had destroyed every conceivable breeding site.

Dr. Surany was at the conference, though there had been pressure to keep him away. If the beetle campaign had a controversial character, it was Surany.

Many of the beetle men had felt that Surany was spending too little time identifying his pathogens and too much time marveling at the damage they did. He had passed too many months peering through microscopes and watching the larva's muscles break down into myofibrils. He had spent too many months holding moribund larvae to the light, like wine, and watching for the last peristalsis of the rectal sac. They felt it was time he stopped traveling the South Pacific and hurried to an electron microscope. Others felt that Surany's work was more promising than anyone's. Owen belonged to the former school. He felt that the time was long past for Surany to concentrate on identifying the disease agents, but he considered Surany a good technician. When Owen heard rumors of the efforts to exclude Surany, he wrote Alexander Kroon to urge that Surany be invited. Everyone with beetle experience should be there, he said. Surany came, and showed hundreds of slides in livid color of his work. Owen found them interesting.

Owen's paper on vegetative barriers was received warmly. It stirred strong arguments both ways. Everyone chipped in his own observations on situations where barrier vegetation seemed to limit beetle damage. Gordon Dunn remembered that in an analogous situation, in the cacao plantations of New Britain, barrier vegetation hindered cacao pests. Dr. Surany remembered that in Sumatra heavy groundcover seemed to prevent female rhinoceros beetles from ovipositioning in what otherwise would have been good breeding media. At the end of the debate, only Dr. Surany, ever the disease advocate, was strongly against experimenting with barriers, which he thought were a waste of time. The first recommendation of the Suva conference was that the barrier idea be tested. Owen was granted £720 for the first year of experiments.

THE CONFERENCE ended, and the beetle fighters dispersed. Owen left the company of men like himself and returned to Palau. From distant corners of the Pacific the beetle fighters would continue to correspond, and in that way would work together while apart, but for Owen the effort was again largely solitary. He knew that while he organized his barrier experiments, T. V. Venkatraman was poking around in elephant droppings somewhere. Hoyt was in Africa and Bianchi in South America. "I am not pleased with the way my *ruficornis* are going," Simmonds would write from Samoa. "Numbers have fallen very much at Dravo, and I am getting very few fresh cocoons." Pemberton, writing from Hawaii, would confess that "I see absolutely no reason why *Pyrophorus pellucens* should not be introduced into Palau and am embarrassed to think that we have not already tried species of the genus." But this was not the same as the conversations at the Grand Pacific Hotel.

Perhaps for Owen there was a letdown in having met his colleagues at last. A distance now came between them that imagination could no longer bridge, for now they had seen and touched one another.

The Pacific is a vast place, and today Owen is not precisely sure which of his coworkers are alive and which are dead.

The men had not met long enough to know one another well. In Owen's letters there was a stiffness, even with men he liked and admired. Several months after the conference, Owen heard that Alexander Kroon was leaving the SPC. "I guess the time is close when you will be leaving the South Pacific Commission," Owen wrote to Kroon. "I am sorry you are leaving. I very much enjoyed my association with you, both when you were in the Trust Territory and Fiji. My wife and I were both thinking of you recently when we spent a week at the Botanic Gardens in Bogor, Java. I think you will be glad to know that the gardens, herbarium, museum and library are being well maintained, though other things in the country seem mostly in confusion."

Kroon was touched, and a little surprised it seems, by Owen's letter.

"It was nice of you and your kind wife to think of me when visiting the Botanic Gardens in Bogor," Kroon wrote. "In 1933, when the Department of Economic Affairs was housed in the buildings near the main entrance of the Gardens, I had to pass through the Gardens four times a day on my way from my house to my office and back. I spent many Sundays with my wife in the Gardens and know the many botanical treasures and beauty spots there. I am certainly very pleased to know that the Gardens are still being well maintained.

"Thank you for your kind words regarding our cooperation. I can assure you that I too enjoyed that association very much and have the most pleasant remembrance of my short stay in Koror."

So the two men were like ships that passed in the Pacific. They hailed one another from a distance, each full of interest in the other, but with greetings muted by distance and convention; and then they parted ways.

9

THE BEETLE WAR has had no satisfactory climax. By 1962 the insect was under control in Palau, but Owen could not be certain to what extent his own efforts were responsible. This was a problem for all beetle fighters. Owen's scolid wasps had spread, undeniably. Their cocoons were being recovered from all parts of Palau. But there was no way to prove that their impact had been substantial. Owen's vegetative barriers seemed to have an effect, and he succeeded in making it a Trust Territory requirement that all homesteaders include barriers in their seedling plantations, but he could not prove the effectiveness of the barriers in an incontestable way. He was not even sure how they worked. It was possible that their effect was to block the beetle's sensory perception of the palm crowns rather than to block the beetle physically, though Owen didn't think so. And it might have been the Palauan ecosystem that had made the real adjustment to the beetle. It takes time for native predators to learn that an exotic arrival is good to eat. A delayed reaction by the environment, in the discovery by monitor lizards, rats, and pigs that beetle larvae taste good, was surely in part responsible for the decrease in beetle damage. How much was due to Owen and how much to ecosystem was hard to say. It was impossible for one entomologist with a dozen helpers to gauge the forces at play in 188 square miles of island jungle.

In Owen's barrier experiments, both a neglected plot where native vegetation was allowed to spring up among the palms, and a second plot where leguminous trees were planted as a barrier, suffered less beetle damage than a third plot kept conventionally bushed, but the difference was not spectacular. It was difficult to design experimental plots that would produce incontestable proof, and Owen was not particularly eager for such proof, anyway. He is not a man anxious for recognition. He knew himself that the barriers helped against the beetle, and that was enough for him. He was not driven to demonstrate it to the world. After Suva, Owen's personal war with the beetle ran downhill. Some of the fire left his relationship with the insect.

The United Nations entered the beetle wars in 1961 and immediately appropriated sums of money that made the South Pacific Commission's original one-year grant of £10,000 look very small. It was wonderful what a little money did; scientists who had resigned themselves to years of impasse now felt the flush of it. Some of them began talking of eradication again.

Much promising work on chemical attractants and chemosterilants has followed the entry of the UN. The new research has turned up a virus disease that, in Owen's opinion, is the best biological control to date. Sanitation remains the basic method of control, however. The victory over the beetle remains in doubt. The beetle waits in the wings for typhoons as potent as Opal and Louise, which in 1964 killed thousands of Palauan palms, providing breeding logs for countless larvae and forcing Owen to start from scratch.

The beetle waits for another war.

Although Owen was confident from the beginning that the beetle's history would run this way, still the inconclusiveness might have been hard for him if the beetle war had been his whole life. It was not. Throughout the beetle years there were other duties, and other fields of science always beckoned him. There were melonflies in the Marianas. There was a mysterious palm disease on Guam. There were epidemics of breadfruit disease in the Ponape district. Owen was responsible for the entomology of three million square miles of ocean. The tiny islands of Micronesia were his scattered domain. He knew Pingelap, Rota, Woleai, Eauripik, Ifaluk, Lamotrek, Kapingamarengi, Mokil, Lapalap, Namu, Kili, Mili, Jaluit, Likiep, Ebon, Faraulep, and others. Often Owen's field-trip ship was at sea for three weeks or more, its doctors and administrators visiting numerous islands when Owen was needed only at one. But he disembarked at each, sometimes turning up problems where there had been no complaints, and always, when not working professionally as an economic entomologist, learning for his own benefit. At countless lagoons of call, on coral islands so small that he could circumambulate them in an hour or less, he indulged his interest in all biology.

One time, anxious to get six hundred lady beetles to the Mortlock Islands, Owen chartered a plywood trimaran. It was an ill-fated boat, twice-wrecked, but his lady beetles were dying and he had no choice. "It's like the U.S. Mail," Owen says. "The bugs have got to get through." His navigator across one hundred sixty miles of open ocean was a Lamotrek man in a loincloth. The trimaran was hit by a storm, and Owen was sure they were doomed. "A trimaran has the goddamned funniest motion," he says. "It dances around. The waves were huge, and each time I saw a big one coming, I told myself this one's going to be it. But the trimaran just floated up and over."

Another time, as he put ashore in a ship's boat on an uninhabited island, Owen was dumped into the surf. He swam safely to shore, but seventeen dollars were washed from his pocket. He tried unsuccessfully to claim the money from the Trust Territory government.

Once Owen was called to Pingelap to study an infection of the island's breadfruit trees. More than half of Pingelap's trees had been killed. Owen called the infection Pingelap disease, and the name took. The disease has since spread to other islands, or at least its presence has been noted on others. The organism that causes the disease, if indeed an organism is responsible, has not been identified, and today Pingelap disease comes and goes. Certain varieties of breadfruit on Pingelap seemed less susceptible, and Owen could only recommend that these be planted in larger numbers.

"I stayed ten days on the island, and I got to know everybody there. There were two hundred people or so. I was the first white man, I guess, to spend that much time with them. I lived in the chief's house. They called him king. His house was made of coral blocks—the only two-story house on the island. They fed me like royalty.

"Toward the end of my stay, the king came to me and told me his problem with money. The people had no safe place for their copra money.

Most of it was paper currency, and the rats ate it, or the people just lost it. The king wanted me to bank the wealth of the island.

"So I spent my last day on the island sitting at a table while the people brought me their money. Some guy would come up with six dollars and thirty-seven cents. But a few of them had hundreds of dollars. I wrote down everyone's name and the amount, and gave the king a receipt. Then I left the island with the money in a sack."

The people of Pingelap, who had never seen movies, were not alarmed by Owen's movie-gambler's face, and they trusted him with the gross monarchal product of many years' labor, but when Owen tried to deposit the $1,295 he carried in his sack, the Bank of America in Guam protested that it couldn't possibly bank something like that. There were too many names. Owen suggested that they put it in the chief's name. That would be irregular, the bank said.

"I finally deposited it myself, and sent a check back to the district administrator of Ponape," Owen says. "I asked him to cash it and put the money on the next field-trip ship to Pingelap. The administrative people in Ponape gave me hell. How could I have done such a thing? I had exceeded my authority. Did I realize I could have absconded with the money? But in the end the money got back to Pingelap. I guess the people understood."

Once Owen hitched a ride on the *Mia Mia,* a ketch owned by a Melbourne man, to Helen Reef, an uninhabited island three hundred miles to the southwest of Palau. Helen Reef is a place magically abundant with turtles, fish, and seabirds. It is occasionally visited by poaching Okinawan fishing boats, and Owen wanted to check on the island's well-being. Helen Reef was in good shape, he found.

On the return voyage the ketch stopped at the island of Merir. This island, along with the four other Southwest Islands—Sonsorol, Pulo Ana, Tobi, and Helen Reef—are included in the Palau district, presumably under the assumption that someone must rule them, but the few inhabitants speak a language different from Palauan and are a different people. When the *Mia Mia* had anchored off Merir, an outrigger canoe came out to greet her— a surprise, for Merir is normally uninhabited. Paddling the canoe was a Palauan from Koror named Kurteribis. He had been left on Merir, he told

Owen, by a field-trip ship several months before, with the understanding that the ship would return for him in a few days. Then there had been a medical emergency on another of the Southwest Islands, Kurteribis guessed, for the ship had sailed directly for Koror without him. Being marooned in this way is common enough on field trips and is a risk everyone takes. Micronesians know how to live alone on small islands. Their tradition prepares them for such holes in their lives, or keeps such interludes from being holes, and it prepares the families back home for long absences.

Kurteribis reported that besides himself there were eleven other Micronesians, all residents of Sonsorol and Tobi, and ten shipwrecked Indonesians on the island. Kurteribis said he spoke a little Indonesian and had been able to learn that the Indonesians were crew members of the *Harapan Islam,* an 80-foot, 150-ton sailing vessel that was bound from Suribaja in Java to Manado on the Celebes island of Sulawesi, carrying a cargo of salt, when she was struck by a storm and sank. The crew escaped in the *Harapan Islam*'s lifeboats, which were simply dugout canoes equipped with sails. Twelve days later, two of the canoes descried Merir and put ashore. The fate of a third canoe was unknown.

The year was 1969, but certain things do not change in Owen's part of the Pacific. There sailing men are still shipwrecked on small islands. In 1970 another group of Indonesian castaways washed up on Merir. They lived on fish and turtle eggs until some Tobi Islanders found them and took them off. Palau was settled in this manner. The migrations of Pacific peoples are still underway, and these latest castaways will not be the last. Other voyagers will leave mounds of empty turtle shells on Merir as their monuments.

When the *Mia Mia* returned to Koror, Owen submitted a routine report to Palau's district administrator. There was no friction between the Indonesians and the Southwest Islanders, Owen reported, but all their store-bought food was gone. The owner of the ketch had left forty pounds of rice, forty pounds of flour, twelve pounds of sugar, and twelve cans of evaporated milk. The Micronesians offered payment, but the owner had refused it. Owen noted that the two Micronesian women on the island were pregnant, one seven months and the other eight, and that both wished to come to Koror's hospital.

76

"All the Micronesians on Merir wish to leave Merir as soon as possible," Owen wrote. "The Indonesians also wish to leave Merir, and the U.S. and Indonesian governments should be made aware of their plight." Owen then listed the names of the Indonesian sailors. Besides Hadji Abdullal, the captain, there were Gudde, Guaepa, Husaen, Lodai, Pangaugro, Sabaiuddin, Safri, Hawsal, and Wirabaja.

OF ALL THE ISLANDS Owen has come to know, he thinks the Palaus are most beautiful. There is more biology in his home district than he can ever learn, more islands than he will ever set foot on. In his wanderings in Palau, Owen has discovered new insect species. He and his wife have explored hidden valleys in certain of the larger elabaob islands and have dug there into the middens of Palauan prehistory. Owen has dived among coral reefs more varied and beautiful than any in the world.

Underwater once, Owen felt, pressing in upon him, a noise he had never heard before, nor has heard since. He turned and saw an army of bump-head parrotfish approaching. He crouched behind a coral head and watched. The army passed by him in a three-dimensional formation. The dorsal fins of the highest fish broke the surface and stood in the sun, and the ventral fins of the lowest brushed the bottom. The noise that enveloped him was the grinding of teeth in thousands of mouths. Owen crouched behind his coral boulder, afraid to betray his position. Parrotfish are a big but vaguely comic species that he had often speared individually without thinking a thing about it, yet now he was uneasy. He had never heard rumor of such a gathering, nor could he imagine what it was for. He watched as the unexpected mystery, the vast potential, of his world passed before him.

BUT WHEN Owen returns from the farther fields of biology, the rhinoceros beetle is waiting for him. His history and the beetle's are intertwined. Their last ten years together have been a standoff, but it will not necessarily always be so, and today in Owen's office insect boxes full of pinned beetles still decorate the walls like wanted posters.

Owen believes that quarantine is only a holding action. Sooner or later the rhinoceros beetle will spread to other islands of the Trust Territory. The longer that is delayed, the more time entomologists will have to improve control methods; but Owen knows that someday, sorting his mail, he will come upon an urgent cablegram and open it to read that the beetle has appeared in Truk or the Marshalls. It will be Demei Otobed's responsibility then, for Demei is now chief entomologist, but it will happen, and Owen has prepared contingency plans for the day. The war will really have begun, for the coconut means everything to inhabitants of low islands.

Owen knows how it will feel, for he has opened just such a cablegram. In it, the director of agriculture for the Marshalls, a man named Cowan, reported what appeared to be beetle damage in several Marshallese palms. A letter followed the cablegram, with a description of the damaged palm and a further piece of evidence: "Mr. Neal Sullivan, Weather Bureau employee, stated that while he was on duty at the weather station he noticed a large 'shiny' insect about two inches long. His first impression was that the bug was a large cockroach, but he noticed that this insect 'lumbered' along as he moved, unlike the fast movements of the cockroach. Mr. Sullivan then struck the insect with a crowbar and kicked it from the top of the building to the ground."

That Sullivan felt obliged to hit the lumbering insect with a crowbar was perhaps the most disturbing detail of all, the strongest suggestion that *O. rhinoceros* had moved to new pastures. The high commissioner's office asked for Owen's opinion and then cabled Cowan. COWAN X TAKE MEASURES TO IDENTIFY SUSPECTED RHINOCEROS BEETLE DAMAGE SOON X REPORT FINDINGS TO OWEN X DO NOT BE SO VAGUE X IMMEDIATE ACTION MANDATORY.

Cowan cabled back. He had uncovered evidence that most of the trees had been mechanically damaged. Aparently the Marshallese had considered the trees undesirable and had cut off the terminal shoots with heavy knives. But in three of the trees, Cowan said, the damage pattern on the fronds was very similar to that of figure 40A, on page 82 of Dr. Gressit's monograph on the beetle. Cowan requested that Owen come to the Marshalls as soon as possible. Between the lines of Cowan's cable there was another cable, reading something like this: DO NOT BE VAGUE? X JESUS CHRIST X AM NOT AN ENTOMOLOGIST X LOOKS JUST LIKE BEETLE DAMAGE IN BOOK TO ME X

DOES ANYBODY KNOW THIS STUFF? X SEND OWEN ASAP. Owen traveled to the Marshalls and studied the damaged trees. He announced that the injury was mechanical. There had been a false alarm, and everything was fine, for now.

Owen and the rhinoceros beetle have lived a curious symbiosis. It would seem that in Owen's view of his own life, the beetle should figure as horned nemesis or at least as fond enemy. It did seem so, at any rate, to a friend who sat and drank with Owen one evening, watching the declining light on the elabaob hills beyond his bungalow. The friend asked Owen if he ever felt sentimental about the beetle; did he ever say to himself that, but for this small insect, he would be in Hoboken? It was the kind of question that Owen finds foolish. No, Owen said, he never felt sentimental. The friend thought it was a good question and he persisted. Then what *would* Owen have done, back in 1949, if the beetle had not been in Palau?

"I would have written a different report," Owen said. "There are lots of insect pests in Palau, you know." He smiled his villainous smile.

"I would have found another insect."

~ 10

ROBERT OWEN arrived in Palau at the only time an American could have had a career there. He came shortly after the Japanese left and twenty years before Palauans began to take over. His life in his chosen islands has been sandwiched neatly between. At the same time, though, Owen has been one of the few Americans to contract hookworm.

"I got it squatting in the bush on Babeldaob. You stay there for two minutes and the cysts are activated and they enter your feet. Pretty soon I had thousands of the little animals with their tiny jaws hooked to my stomach wall, sucking my lifeblood. I was a classic case. My breath smelled bad. I was listless, pale, anemic. I went out to the airfield to greet the high commissioner once and he was afraid to shake my hand. I was tottering. I was sick for a year before they told me at the Guam hospital what I had. They tried to test my blood. The nurse told me I didn't have any. Then they gave me a capsule and the effect was instantaneous. It was like taking off an eighty-pound pack after you've been walking all day. It was a big horse capsule. Hydrocarbon, you know. I tasted gasoline for a week, but I just floated."

All of fate's kindly dispensations to Owen have this flip side. Providence was looking after him when, the day after he left Carthage, his captured Volkswagen command car was destroyed in the crash landing of a shot-up plane, and Providence was watching over him all the times he himself landed in shot-up planes. But Providence took terrible care of his snake collection. A mix of good luck and bad is predictable in any life, of course, but for Owen, more clearly than for most, the luck seems to follow from the nature of his choices.

"In Palau I've had the opportunity to indulge in all biology," he says. "My bosses have been a thousand miles away. I've been doing things that no one in the Trust Territory understands or has any competence in." But there has been another side to this freedom; in his separation from men who understand him, Owen has been alone.

Biologists sometimes do stop in Palau. Several of the beetle fighters called on Owen there. E. M. Nicholson visited, and Maurice Yonge, leader of the Great Barrier Reef expeditions, and Thomas Goreau, perhaps the world's foremost student of coral reefs. Owen has met more great men in Palau, he believes, than he would have met if he had stayed in the States. But if the quality has been high, quantity is sometimes thin.

"I couldn't live in Palau without the stimulation of talk with scientists," Owen says. "I'm a blotter. I soak up what these people are thinking. I've learned a hell of a lot from them."

Owen reads, but his magazines and books usually arrive late. Reading is not enough, anyway. Owen needs the conversation. If Owen left it up to the scientists, too few of them would come to keep him in the islands, so Owen has not left it up to them. He is a man remarkably skillful, most of the time, at shaping his own fate. The laboratory hilltop, with its lawn, lily pond, and surrounding botanical garden—its few acres of order imposed on the jungle—is a measure of the order he can impose on his life. Faced with a shortage of scientists, Owen set out deliberately to attract them. Above the biology lab he built an apartment for visitors. He observes that academic men are generally timid about traveling. The prospect of a place as rich biologically as Palau, yet so remote and primitive, leaves them excited but uncomfortable. The word *apartment* for these people is reassuring. In his letters of invitation Owen describes the apartment's refrigerators and the laboratory's facilities. He describes the boats available. Scientists come and are glad that they did. They depart having served Owen in two ways: they have investigated and will publicize Palau's natural history—Owen believes that to be saved, Palau's biota must be known—and they have kept Owen in touch. In the Trust Territory government, men talk of the "rock fever" of colleagues who stay in the field too long. Owen does not want that malady creeping up on him.

The guest scientists often leave Palau without knowing how much they mean to Owen. From his bungalow Owen could hit the apartment's corrugated-metal roof with a rock, but he seldom visits the men and women living there. His conversation with his guests need not be frequent. Their proximity is enough, apparently. They seem to serve him as an absent soldier's photograph serves his mother, or as talismans.

But Owen's mastery of his fate has not been total. Sometimes the apartment is vacant.

FROM TIME TO TIME in the Trust Territory there have been resident scientists whom Owen admired. One was a man named Pieris, with a wonderful title: Director of Coconut Operations. Pieris and Owen were enemies of sorts. The Director of Coconut Operations was strongly against Owen's vegetative-barrier idea because of what he considered "the evil effects of the presence of secondary jungle on the vegetative and reproductive performance of coconut palms."

"Dick Pieris was an arrogant guy," Owen says. "He was a Singhalese from Ceylon. A typical one. The only two races I can't seem to get along with are the French and Ceylonese. I liked him.

"Pieris had a degree from Cambridge. He dressed like a gentleman, all real natty. He had a fetish about personal cleanliness. He worried about bacteria. I would sleep with the natives, but Pieris wouldn't. He had a whole safari outfit. Tent. Foldable table. Collapsible bar. I was on Laura once, in Majuro Atoll, when Pieris was there. I didn't know he was on the island until he sent a boy over and invited me for drinks. I walked to his camp. My clothes were all worn. I was filthy. There was Pieris, standing coolly at his bar. 'What'll you have, Bob? Scotch? A martini?'

"Pieris wouldn't eat the native food. The people all laughed at him."

But Pieris had one quality that might have made Owen's life in the

Pacific easier, had Owen possessed it. Pieris was black. He was a Singhalese of medium height and a little chubby, with the very smooth skin of his people, and he was very dark, darker than the average Palauan.

"One thing he did that really teed me off," Owen recalls. "It was on his first trip to Palau. We were touring the villages, giving lectures about the beetle. We talked about planting and thinning coconut plantations. He was a good speaker. He had a good speaking presence, with lots of gestures and pauses. I was the only *haole* there—the only white man. 'You know you can believe what I say,' Pieris told them, 'because I am from an island, *and my skin is black, like yours.*' "

The letters Pieris wrote in opposition to Owen's vegetative barriers were forceful and well written. Their argument might have made trouble for the barriers, Owen thinks, had it not been so eloquent. The communications from DIRCOPRA TERPACIS, which was Pieris's fine-sounding cable address, to HICOMPTERPACIS, the office of the high commissioner of the Trust Territory of the Pacific Islands, were often twelve pages long. The memos from DIRENT TERPACIS, who was Robert Owen, were shorter and easier to read. Pieris may have sensed this, but he was not able to modify his style. Toward the end of his losing struggle with the barriers, badly entangled himself in Owen's secondary vegetation, Pieris wrote, "I regret that in what may well be my last days in the Trust Territory my scientific conscience still drives me to assume the characters of Jeremiah and Cassandra rolled in one, 'uncowed by fear or favour of the crowd!' "

That was too rich for the plain American folks back at headquarters. Pieris left the Trust Territory government, in part because of the barrier controversy. Owen had won, but now he missed the conversations with Pieris in the field and the arguments at each other's house.

Years later Pieris wrote Owen from the Far East, giving the latest news and asking for some cocoons of *S. ruficornis*. The cocoon request amused Owen, for Pieris had been very cool to the wasp when he was Director of Coconut Operations. Owen answered that he would be in the Far East soon himself and that "if our paths cross during this time, I think that it might be interesting if we could get together and spar a few more words on coconuts and their insects. I don't think that I picked your brain completely when you were in the Trust Territory, and there might be a couple of little items that you didn't find in mine."

TODAY THERE ARE a few Palauan scientists in Palau, for American colleges are returning a sprinkling of Micronesians to their native islands. Demei Otobed, who began as Owen's employee and who presently, as Chief Entomologist, shares the biology lab with him, has attended universities in the Philippines and Hawaii. Otobed is now a better trained entomologist than Owen, as Owen himself admits. It might seem that in Otobed Owen would find the scientific companionship he requires, and to an extent he does. The two biologists sit across the desk from one another and exchange thoughts over the mound of papers there. They were drinking companions in the days when Otobed drank. Demei is closer to Owen than any other Palauan man. Yet the two remain worlds apart.

Demei is in the Modekgnie religion. He is not a member in good standing—he smokes and uses sugar—but he wishes that he were. He would like to believe with his whole heart, as his father does, but he can't. He is a man caught between cultures. In his schooling abroad he has been exposed to Western systems of thought, and these have become, to an extent, his own systems.

Demei would like to believe in magic.

"The magician cuts off the growing tip of the ti plant," he explains with animation in the lab office one afternoon. "The magician lays it on the ground and makes a circle around it with his arms. He says all kinds of things to that ti plant. He chants to it and so forth. Then he begins naming all the possible causes of death. When he hits the correct one, the ti plant begins to dance and tremble. If it dances over and touches the magician's arm, then the magician begins to tremble too. I have never seen it myself, but my father has."

The school solution is that if magic works, it works through suggestion. There is more to it than this, Demei believes, but how much more, he can't say.

Demei deeply respects his father's unlettered wisdom. "Don't go to sea. Stay on land," his father said enigmatically once as Demei was about to depart with John Kochi on a patrol for poachers. For Demei the words had oracular force. He stayed on land.

Demei feels the fascination of the idea of royalty. That certain Palauans are powerful by accident of birth is of great interest to him—more so than to Kochi, who simply calls such people "fat cats." The present ibedul, the most powerful chief in Palau, often drinks with younger men and does not maintain the proper distance, in Demei's opinion, but you must remember that he is ibedul. If, sitting beside the ibedul at the bar, you say something that displeases him, he fines you. He can fine you in American money, which is bad, but also in Palauan money, which is worse, for it exists in a fixed amount and can only be a deflationary currency. The ibedul knows which pieces of Palauan money your family owns. If he demands them, your family must pay. Demei smiles at the raw power of this, ruefully but with pleasure, as one does when someone on the other team hits a very long ball.

Once a visitor to the laboratory remarked that the Latin name for Palau's littoral crab, *Graspus,* was a good one. "Our name is better," Demei replied. "The Palauan word is more descriptive. We call the crab *rereek,* which means a shuffling noise. Like if someone in another room is handling papers. The crabs sound exactly like that when they are moving over rocks." When there is a Palauan version, Demei prefers it.

During school vacation Demei holds a botany class for Palauan teachers in the laboratory insectary. In the course of his lectures he holds up leaves of the various species he is describing. When he has no demonstration leaf, Demei evokes the missing shape with gestures of his hands, and the mimed leaf's outlines become as real as if he held it by the stem. Demei lectures on osmotic pressure. His hand undulates upward with a sewing motion, lifting the water up through the stalk, against the resistance, against the terrible pull of gravity. Somehow the climbing hand conveys all the plant's urgency. Then suddenly water is scarce. Demei's hand undulates downward again, his voice descending the scale, and the plant shuts down its operations. When Demei lectures on the oxygen problems faced by mangroves and other tidal species, he pauses in the middle to hold his breath, pinch his nose, and look desperately up at the surface of the high tide above him. Lecturing on asexual reproduction in plants, he makes a joke in Palauan, and the class laughs.

Demei's gift as a teacher is a Palauan gift, acquired during a subsistence boyhood spent close to the life of plants. But sometimes in the lecture there is no Palauan word for what Demei wants to say, and of necessity fragments of English litter his sentences. "An epiphyte growing on top of . . . organic matter . . . a specialized leaf, a tendril . . . produce acids which dissolve the rock . . ." and other such phrases mar his Palauan rhythm. Demei hurries past, giving the English words as little weight as he can.

When Owen is away, Demei is in charge of the biology laboratory, but foreign visitors to the office never seem to sense this. If a white scientist is working there, the visitors walk past the small brown man, Demei, and stop at the scientist's desk. When the scientist confesses that he is a visitor here himself, and indicates Demei as the man of authority, they turn to him, but it is too late. Demei's answers to their questions are clipped and cold. The visitors leave quickly, without knowing what they have done, or knowing only dimly.

When a guest scientist is new to the office he sometimes sits in Demei's chair. Demei's anger on returning to the room is contained but palpable, filling the air like the lab's odor of formalin. (The day Demei stepped as a student from the plane in Hawaii, the first thing he noticed was that native Hawaiians were sweeping up the airport and driving the cabs. White men were running the show. For Demei that was real education, a bite of green apple, and he remembers the taste.) The scientist never sits in Demei's chair again. Demei always regrets his anger and tries to soften it. He knows that he has made a symbolic act of an innocent one; that this individual white man is not his enemy. In his stiff way he makes amends.

So it is not so much that Owen and Otobed are products of different cultures that separates them. Neither is any longer very representative of his people. Otobed accepts Darwinian evolution, and Owen accepts magic. But Owen is the colonial officer and Otobed is the native. That relationship, like the one between master and servant, is never so simple as either party pretends.

ROBERT OWEN courted Hera Ware in a 1913 Model T that he backed up the steep hill to her door. He kept the differential full of sawdust and the crankcase full of discarded oil. Hera made him listen to harpsichord music, he remembers. He remembers her dressed in green stockings, feeding him cucumbers under the Montlake bridge in Seattle. They first kissed under a red light in the darkroom of a photography class at the University of Washington. Later Hera studied under Martha Graham and worked with modern dance troupes in New York. Today, in Palau, she still speaks wonderingly of Miss Graham's discipline, stage presence, and genius. Hera Ware Owen was a liberated sort, a good match for young Owen, the bat hunter in black homburg. She was ready to accompany her husband to one of the ends of the earth. But Hera Owen is not a biologist, and in Palau she does not enter her husband's professional solitude.

When Hera explains her husband, it is almost in terms of dance. His visual judgment and timing are exceptional, she says. He has not fired a rifle more than a dozen times in their life together, but each time he does he startles her with his accuracy. Snake hunting with him, she has been surprised at how deft and quick his hands are. His skill is a combination of physical gifts and his knowledge of snakes, she thinks. She is confident of his ability to anticipate and handle larger animals too, and she feels secure in wild places with him. Once in her early years in Palau, Hera watched while her husband speared two crocodiles in the family's swimming cove, and then she and her children went swimming. Her husband has very good eyes, she says, and he can identify birds at great distances. He becomes very clear thinking in danger. She believes that this quality, along with his eyesight and quick reactions, was what kept him alive in his Martin Marauder.

"My husband had a very close friend named Sid Seid, who was a pilot," Hera remembers. "Not a pilot in the war, but here in Palau. One day Sid went off in a small plane to search for a missing fishing boat, and he never returned. Bob often tells me he wishes that he had been on the plane. Sid was a good pilot, but Bob believes if he had been there he might have moved quickly enough, or thought quickly enough, to save them."

LATER THAT EVENING Owen sits in his living room with a scotch and water in his hand. Below the hilltop the waters of Iwayama Bay catch the last light of day. Owen's windows have wire screens, not glass, and the evening breezes and evening noises enter easily. Owen cocks his head and listens. From out of a general piping of tree frogs he picks the occasional squeak of a fruit bat. He smiles.

His wife enters the room and moves to the door to close it.

"Leave the door open, Hera," Owen says. "There are no bugs around here. This is the entomologist's house."

Owen sips his scotch and listens to the frogs. Palau's shy, fast-moving tree frogs have no tadpole stage. They give birth to live young. Owen believes this may be an adaptation to the elabaob islands, whose limestone is so porous that rainfall drains off immediately, leaving no standing fresh water for tadpoles to grow up in.

The bungalow door, which opens on the hilltop lawn, remains ajar, and through it Owen can see a dusky patch of sky. Bats are hunting for insects in the red rectangle. Owen suddenly turns to his wife. "You know, this insectivorous bat we're seeing is endemic to Palau," he tells her. "It occurs nowhere else." He quickly and apologetically gives the bat's scientific name. He seems to have just realized, surprised, that he has never told Hera this in their twenty-odd years in the islands.

THE PALAUAN PEOPLE do not like Owen. Their dislike is not much of a personal indictment, for of all the Americans in the Micronesian government, there is only one man of whom Palauans sometimes speak approvingly, and there is no consensus about him. The Palauan people half-wish that Owen and the other Americans in Palau would pack up and leave, but Palauans have been taught, and have come to believe, that they are not ready yet to govern themselves. Angry young Palauans believe this along with the rest, and it compromises their militancy. So the Palauan people put up with Owen, but they complain a lot about him.

"What has Owen done for us?" asks a young woman of high clan, educated abroad. She is a big, hearty woman in the old tradition of Oceanic queens, and she is destined by birth to be powerful in Palau. She can drink Owen under the table, Owen confesses, and he is very fond of her. "Bob Owen came twenty-five years ago because of the coconut beetle," she continues. "We still have the beetle. And we still have Owen, up there in his little kingdom on the hill. What has he been doing?"

When Palauans are stung by wasps they blame Owen, remembering that he introduced the scolid wasp in the fight against the beetle. The scolid wasp is not in fact the species that is stinging them, and Demei Otobed, never an apologist for Owen, is moved by fairness and concern for scientific accuracy to point this out. "I was personally stung by wasps before Owen came, so how can it be his fault?" Demei asks, but this is not something his countrymen want to hear.

Palauans remember Owen and the short-lived rhinoceros-beetle-bounty program. The bounty system was a Palauan colonial tradition when Owen came. The Japanese had made much use of bounties in their efforts to control Palau's rats, snails, and other pests, and the Palauan people liked their system. In 1956, at a time when Owen was absent from the islands, a number of Palauan leaders convinced an assistant district administrator that a beetle-larva contest would be a good idea. A bounty would be paid for *Oryctes* larvae, the official decreed, and whichever village collected the most would win a prize. Drums of beetle larvae began to arrive at the biology lab. The drums made Owen unhappy. He would never have recommended a bounty himself. He knew that when American Samoa had experimented with a bounty system for beetles, the Samoans had begun raising larvae for sale, carefully protecting them from their pigs. Larva farms like those of Samoa, if carelessly tended, would become dangerous breeding sources in Palau. Owen worried, also, that the areas where his scolid wasp program was getting started would be invaded and disturbed by larva hunters. And when he examined the drums sent to him, he found that thousands of the larvae were of beetles other than *Oryctes*. This was the wrong way to spend the people's energies, Owen thought. On his complaint, the district administrator aborted the program, but drums of assorted decomposing larvae continued to arrive at the lab. The Palauans were angry when Owen refused to pay.

"He has only sweet talk, but his heart is bending like a hook," the ibedul is reported to have said of Owen. This sounds like something Cochise or Sitting Bull might have said, and as such it has a convincing ring. It may in fact be true. But Ibedul Ngeriakl is not a noble-savage sort of chief. He is a shrewd and wealthy businessman, and there are often things to read between his lines.

Palauans *do* watch their Americans closely, however, with a ruthless sort of pleasure. Natives seem to know more about colonial administrators than the other way around, and the Palauans have been studying Robert Owen for a long time. No Palauan believes that Owen's actions are ever simple and without motive. Owen is smart, the Palauan Owen-watchers say. Owen knows that his face and personality do not shine with a boyish honesty, and he uses John Kochi to make up for that. Kochi, in his straightforwardness, is the perfect cover for a devious man. Owen is generous in his praise of Kochi and Otobed because he thinks he can control them. By advancing them to positions of power he is entrenching for the day Palauans take over. Kochi and Otobed will be his Palauan faces.

Because Owen is a private man, it is hard to know from talking to him how much of the criticism is fair. His correspondence files are full of letters to Palauans that seem to reveal real feeling for them. He is a better correspondent, at least, than the Palauans he sends away to school. There is a plaintive note common to many of the letters. "We're proud of your performance. Please acknowledge the Trust Territory news material we've been sending you," he wrote to James Remarii, who was attending forestry school in New Guinea. "Tell me how you are getting along," he wrote Takesi Suzuki, who was learning scientific draftsmanship in Hawaii. "Demei said you saw a large sea snake (Mengirnger) when you were in South Palau. On what island or on what part of the island did you see the snake?" The Owen-watchers know about such letters but are not impressed.

Palauans do not like Owen, but they know him. Other Americans come and go, but Owen is always there. He has been in the service of the Trust Territory longer than any other man. He is an institution, and Palauans are comfortable with him. Sometimes the relationship works well. One of the innovations of which Owen is proudest, the council-of-chiefs conservation program, was worked out with the assistance of John Kochi and Kathy Kesolei of Palau Community Action, and with the cooperation of the chiefs themselves. Owen proposed to the chiefs that they undertake the punishment of conservation-law violators. If the laws were enforced at the village level, Owen hoped, a considerable burden would be lifted from Kochi and the conservation office, and more Palauans would become involved in conservation. If the violator refused to accept the chief's sentence, he would then be tried by the government in Koror, but most would accept the chief's decision. The chiefs liked the idea. Aside from its conservation merits, it was a means of strengthening their eroded power.

Owen has considered becoming a Palauan citizen but has decided against it.

"Changing citizenship wouldn't change me inside. I could stay here another twenty years and I still wouldn't be a Palauan. The thought processes and everything are entirely different. After you've been here a long time the people might say you're a Palauan, but it's always a little tongue in cheek. Sure, it might have been different if I'd come out here single and married a Palauan girl. But in New Caledonia I met an American who had changed his citizenship and become a Cook Islander. He'd married a Cook Island girl. He was thinking about owning property and getting a job. As far as the jobs went, though, his skin color was enough to sink him.

"And it's a big step, changing the citizenship your family has had for generations. Oh, I've thought about it. . . ."

When Owen's return to Palau from a trip in the field brings him through Yap, he buys Yapese betel nut for his staff, but when he gets home he must ask Demei Otobed to translate, telling his men to come for it. After twenty-two years in the islands, Owen does not speak the Palauan language. The Palauans who know him, and American visitors of a more anthropological bent than he, find this more than a little strange. Owen himself is puzzled. "If I were to justify it," he says, "I suppose I would say that my responsibility has been for the whole Trust Territory, not just one group of islands and one language."

For a visitor to the laboratory hilltop, it seems sometimes that it must be obvious to everyone but the protagonists—the Palauans and Owen himself—that Owen loves Palauans. Other times the visitor is not so sure. Given Owen's essential shyness and Palauan suspiciousness, it is unlikely that the visitor, or Owen, or the Palauans, will ever know.

Owen has changed in the Pacific. Once a student with radical notions, he is now, and has been for most of his adult life, the agent of a colonial power. ("We say we're not colonialists, so we don't take the responsibilities of colonialists," he complains of the Trust Territory government.) He genuinely believes that the role of an American government officer in Micronesia should be to work himself out of a job and be replaced as soon as possible by a Micronesian; yet he wants to stay in Palau, so he finds new jobs to work himself out of. Owen is not a natural bureaucrat, and from the beginning he has complained about the bureaucracy of the Micronesian government, but he has learned to be skillful at surviving within that bureaucracy. ("Don't jump into battle swinging, let it die a natural death, if possible," he wrote to a friend in Guam who was resisting the importation of exotic birds.) Owen himself makes mistakes in this regard—once when a proposal was made to study the feasibility of mining phosphate in the elabaob islands, he did not keep his opposition as anonymous as he should have—but he learned from that. He has adopted a caution that is not necessarily natural to him.

Over the years Owen's Palauan staff have slowly changed him, remaking their boss after a Japanese model. Owen is not quite an autocrat, but he is gruffer in his relations with his Palauan subordinates than a younger Owen, the bat hunter in the black homburg, would have been. His Palauan employees have helped him to become that way. They seldom tell Owen what they are thinking. Their teeth smile when they are not smiling inside. If an employee forgets himself and gets angry at Owen, Owen is surprised and apologetic for whatever it is he has done—not at all like the Japanese overseers of the old days. But the employees seldom forget themselves.

Sometimes Owen seems a tragic figure, exiled among people who do not understand him, and whom he does not understand. He seems a man who has paid too great a price for what he thought was paradise. Owen does not feel that way. He always knew, he says, that he would live in a place like Palau. He never finds it strange, dropping out of the clouds on a return flight from the Marshalls or the Marianas or the Eastern Carolines, and seeing again the long, green island of Babeldaob and the jigsaw puzzle of the elabaob islands to the south, that this is home.

Part Two

II

WHEN CHIEF CONSERVATIONIST Robert Owen has a hangover and has not shaved, his face looks scary, and his morning entrance at the biology laboratory office is sour. Demei Otobed, the chief entomologist, enters the office preoccupied. Like most Palauans educated in the West, Otobed has a lot to think about. He is bitter about a number of things, but he is funny. His ready humor is good for the office, for it offsets Owen's occasional sourness. "He should join the comedians," John Kochi has said of his friend. Otobed's humor is bilingual. He can make Americans laugh as well as Palauans. His initials are D.O.O., so he initials his memos DO_2, a small joke lost on most Palauans, among them Kochi. Once Otobed looked up from a monograph he was reading and broke the office silence. "You know, *Rubak,*" he said to Owen, "the sea urchin in Guam is a little bigger than the sea urchin we have here." His tone was earnest, academic. "I wonder if we could get them to breed and produce an average-sized sea urchin?" It was a joke excessively subtle for Palau. Only Owen and Otobed and a handful of others could have appreciated it. Owen smiled.

John Kochi's chair is often empty. As Palau's conservation officer, he spends much of his time in the field. When he does enter, he never just slips in. Owen and Otobed are able to enter unobtrusively, but Kochi cannot. It may be simply that he's big and broad and does not fit so easily through the door. But in Kochi there also seems to be a different kind of radiation, another order of energy.

KOCHI COMES IN from patrol. He is hot and sweating, in a good mood, his teeth bright red from chewing betel nut, his cheek big with the nut and the *kebui* leaf it was wrapped in, his outdoor voice a little too loud for indoors. Entering, he seems to expand in volume. There is apparently a pressure differential—fewer pounds per square inch here in the cool of the office than outside in his Palauan sunshine.

Kochi is excited by something he has just learned from some Okinawans, and he repeats it for his colleagues. According to the Okinawans, sea snakes assemble in "houses" after eating, Kochi says. There are few such houses in the world, and they are very hard to find. Every Okinawan snake hunter dreams of discovering one. Each house must be a sort of grotto, part on land and part in the sea. There must be an underwater entrance, and the chamber on land must open above, so that the snakes can sun themselves. Hundreds of sea snakes, more poisonous than cobras but with mild dispositions, gather there.

"In Okinawa," Kochi says, "there is a man who is a millionaire from finding the sea-snake house. Anyone who finds it gets rich. They sell the hides to the Japanese. They make medicines from the meat. It's good for some diseases they have in Japan."

Owen and Otobed listen with interest, but with reservations. Kochi seems to have none. He is a man who lives in the mind and not the intellect. The idea of breeding an average-sized sea urchin would appeal to him.

In addition to Palauan, Ponapean, Guamanian, and English, Kochi speaks some Japanese, and it was in that language that he conversed with the snake hunters. Kochi is a Japanese name. John's father was either a Japanese or an Okinawan or a Japanese-Okinawan named Kochi Koske. In accordance with Palauan custom John has taken his father's first name as his last. He did not always do so, however. He was raised by a stepfather, a Palauan man named Ngiraingas, and he used that name until recently. John is a church name that only Americans use. His countrymen call him Singer, or less commonly, Singeru. Singer doesn't sound Japanese, but if you question Kochi on that, he will insist that it is: "Sure it's Japanese. You know those sewing machines called Singer? That's a big Japanese company."

John Singer Kochi has a broad, dark face. It is hard to say exactly how dark, for like anyone with dark skin, Kochi changes shade with the light conditions. When you look into the tropical sun at him, he goes very black. Twenty feet underwater, he is pale. At one hundred and fifty feet and deeper—depths to which he sometimes dives—he is probably something else again. His color changes, too, with his company. Standing next to countrymen in whom the Melanesian heritage dominates, Kochi looks diluted, but standing next to Robert Owen, he looks very dark indeed. He is a shade that Europeans often carelessly describe as black. One Afro-American aquaintance of Kochi's, more accustomed than the average European-American at recognizing and naming the various degrees of darkness, has decided he is dark brown.

When you learn that Kochi's father was Japanese, you can see it in Kochi's face. The father is apparent mainly in the samurai arch of the son's eyebrows. Kochi's hours on the water, squinting against the sun, have knitted his brows in a nearly perpetual frown. It gives him a fierce look, like an actor in a sword epic. Above his right eyebrow, near where it meets the bridge of his nose, there is a deep, inch-long nick. This is an American feature; he was cut there in a Fort Benning training accident. Kochi has two versions of how the accident occurred. In one, he overruns the objective in a platoon exercise too eagerly, before the mortars have ceased firing, and is wounded by a fragment. In the other, less colorful, he simply bangs his head against the windshield of a jeep.

Kochi's face is expressive, but less of moods than of levels of energy. When he is tired, his face shows it clearly, and when he is dead tired his face shows that too. Also, and more often, it shows the opposite of fatigue. Kochi's teeth are those of a moderate betel-nut chewer. He does not often use the Japanese-brand smoker's toothpastes with which more vain Palauan betel-nut chewers clean their teeth. Below the cutting edges of his incisors is the dull-red betel-nut patina, telltale, as if Kochi cared.

Kochi's voice seems small for his body. He speaks with a diminished force, as if in past exertions he blew a vocal gasket. His forearms are short and thick, their girth accentuated by the broad leather watchband in which his black-faced diver's watch is set. With certain gestures, as when with elbow on desk he brings a cigarette to his mouth, the forearms seem wider than long. Kochi is approximately thirty-three years old.

Like Robert Owen, John Kochi is an instinctive naturalist. Kochi was born in the Stone Age, or something very close to it. (The fish spear that he used as a boy had metal points, but his way of hurling it was very old and premetallic.) Owen was born in the Machine Age, or whatever that age was called back in 1916. Yet in their approach to the matters that concern them both most profoundly, natural history and conservation, the two men are very alike. Their differences have mostly to do with accident of birth in different epochs and oceans apart. Someday, if all goes well, Kochi will replace Owen as Chief Conservationist for the Trust Territory.

THE AFTERNOONS pass pleasantly in the lab office. The office is air-conditioned to preserve the insect collections, and this makes it a cool and satisfactory place to work. For a newcomer there is an odor of formalin on entering, but none of the lab regulars notice it.

Owen departs to rake some leaves, then returns. He resumes editing one of John Kochi's reports. Kochi's chair is empty. The conservation officer has left again to go patrolling. When Owen has finished revising it, Kochi's report reads fairly well:

"At about 12:00 noon I spotted a wildfire between Imeyong village and Ngeremetengel village. This wildfire started about a mile away from Imeyong village on the roadside close to the mangrove forest and eating up toward Ngeremetengel village. This wildfire may have started at about 10:00 AM that morning and when I arrived it has spread wide up to the savannah burning many wild growing trees, grasses, and bamboo. I have tried to stop the fire in prevention of spreading more but I couldn't make any success in controlling the fire. There was no body in sight so suspected person or persons is or were unknown."

Outside the glass door of the office, four small brown girls are jumping rope. For the pleasure of lawn underfoot, the girls have walked up to the hilltop from the town's nearest shacks. Nina Dlutaoch, Owen's lab assistant, decides to take a break and join them. She walks outside and takes a turn at jumping. Nina is twenty-two and she bounces in a way that little girls don't. Owen looks up, and he watches the jumping with more interest than before. Nina returns laughing and out of breath. She settles into her work again, and the office is quiet for a while.

An argument begins over chiggers. Demei Otobed attacks chiggers and Nina defends them. Otobed dislikes chiggers because, he claims with mock delicacy, "they have a habit of entering your forbidden areas." "*Bulak!*" says Nina. The word means "liar," but it sounds like a stronger American swear word and that's why Nina likes to use it. It's not true about chiggers, she says. There's lots of chiggers on her home island, Peleliu, and she has never heard anyone complain of itching in those places. "Maybe you're immune," says Owen.

"Or maybe," Otobed says, "she doesn't have any forbidden areas." Nina balls up a sheet of paper and throws it at him.

"On January 3," Kochi has written, "I patroled on the eastern part of Babeldaob Island from Koror and when I about reaching Ngerechur Island at the end of Babeldaob Island the 33-hp Johnson motor conked out on me and I have to pole to Chollei Municipality and radio to Koror for help. Help came on January 4 and we all came safetly." Owen corrects a few items, then sets this report with the others. He deliberately leaves a lot of Kochi's flavor in the edited reports. He hopes that someday Kochi will be the man to replace him, but in working toward that end he is careful not to misrepresent Kochi's command of English. He takes up another report, this time an account of a patrol for pigeon poachers.

"I spotted two man standing one within the vegetative barrier and one about a foot deep in the water dressing pigeons before the Yanmar boat reach the beach. These two man on the shore saw me and took off into the vegetative barrier so I did not identify them so I took what ever they left at the beach such as zorries and pigeon feathers."

Nina Dlutaoch takes another break. She walks to the cupboard and fetches a plastic bowl. She pours in soy sauce, adds a lot of salt and two very hot red peppers. She walks out to the *titimel* tree in the lawn, and with a long bamboo she knocks off a number of the small, sour, apple-green fruit. Sitting on the bench outside the office, she cuts the fruit into small pieces, dips them in the bowl, and eats. In Palau it is the fruit of the titimel, not pickles or ice cream, that pregnant women crave. Nina just likes titimel—she always has, she loves sour things—but because of its reputation she avoids eating it at home. When her mother sees her on the roof, eating the fruit under the family's titimel tree, she always demands to know if Nina is pregnant. Nina *is* pregnant, as a matter of fact, though no one else knows it yet.

Outside the office window the sun is shining on the ocean. A storm approaches and darkens the waters for a time. The storm cloud moves north toward Babeldaob, and again the sun burnishes the sea. John Kochi is patrolling out there, somewhere.

At 4:30 the office closes. Nina Dlutaoch leaves first, walking barefoot homeward. Then Robert Owen removes his glasses and rises. He shuffles through his papers, selecting those he will read tonight, and departs, walking across the upper lawn to his bungalow. The jump-rope girls are long gone, and John Kochi has not returned. Demei Otobed is the last to go. He leaves the air-conditioning on for the sake of the insect collections. He padlocks the office door, and then the front gate, and he walks through the heat of evening down the dirt road to town.

~ 12

WHEN SINGER was a boy his hair stuck out so wildly that they called him Sea Urchin. Singer was not a well-behaved boy, his mother remembers. He was a very bad boy, in fact. He threw stones at the Japanese and stole rice from Japanese houses. He was a liar. He refused to do his share of the work. He threatened people.

"A child of the back" in Palau is one who is good always, even when his mother's back is turned. "A child of the front" is bad as soon as he gets the chance. Singer was neither; he was bad always. Early in the American occupation, when he was supposed to be going to school, Singer walked instead to a roadside trash can. He dropped his books in and then climbed in himself. He remained in the can until school was over, standing up when the mood struck him and watching passers-by. When his older sister found him in the can she beat him, but it did no good at all.

Singer's mother, Obeketakl, a dark, broad lady with arms tattooed in black, as was the custom of her generation, has to laugh in the remembering.

Singer's badness was not so very unusual, for he was from Airai, and the young people of Airai Municipality are famous troublemakers. The tradition goes back to Medechibelau, "he-who-grasps-Palau," the god of Airai. Medechibelau was a rogue. His influence persists in the district soil, like DDT, and continues to flower in each new generation. When Medechibelau was a boy and his mother left for the taro fields, he used his magic to fill the house with water. From a hiding place he took the original shark, his pet, and played with it. He would bang on the walls and shout "wu! wu! wu!" to make the shark race around the room. To keep his mother ignorant, he asked her to make some kind of noise when she came home; otherwise, he said, she frightened him. When Medechibelau heard her noise, he reversed his magic, causing the water to vanish, and he hid his shark. Twice his mother made a noise as she was asked, and each time on entering she found the floor wet. Medechibelau explained that he had been cleaning house, but his mother was suspicious. It probably struck her as an unlikely story. On the third afternoon she made no noise and caught her son using the house as an aquarium. Medechibelau was forced to let his shark go, and today its descendants fill the seas. Modern black-tip sharks are still very easily frightened. You need only bang on the floor of your canoe or raft, shout "wu! wu! wu!" and any nearby black-tips will scatter.

Singer was a boy in the Medechibelau mold.

Singer had several brothers, the oldest of whom, Marcellus, was born fifteen years before him. Marcellus was one of the few Palau Islanders whom the Japanese picked to attend school abroad—an honor his family still remembers with pride.

One day of the year Singer was six, Marcellus was returning on a Japanese ship from his studies in Singapore and was gazing over the rail at his home islands, growing steadily larger on the horizon, when he looked up to see American planes. Obeketakl, who was ashore awaiting her son's return, remembers this occasion as "the day the war began." For the people of Palau, it was indeed the beginning, though in less remote parts of the world the fighting had been on for some time. The Japanese ship was attacked and sunk, and Marcellus swam across seven miles of open ocean to Angaur Island.

He was stranded on Angaur longer than he wished. He did not feel that he was home yet. In Palau Islanders, sense of place is highly developed. The people have strong ties to their natal villages. A Palauan woman returns home to give birth so that her child can become imprinted by his place. For Marcellus that place was the southern part of Babeldaob Island, forty miles to the north. At first the Japanese denied his requests, then they granted him permission to return to Babeldaob. He reached home at night, on a transport vessel.

Marcellus was pro-American. This was odd, for Palauans knew very little about America. It is doubtful that Marcellus had ever seen an American. That the Japanese were able to advertise American troops as invaders from Mars is a measure of how little the general populace knew of the outside world, America in particular. Besides, American planes had just sunk a ship under Marcellus. But in Singapore Marcellus must have read about America. He had learned some English. Now, safely home in Palau again, he had long arguments with his sister, who was pro-Japanese. Perhaps Marcellus liked the idea of freedom as it was said to be practiced in America. Or maybe he liked the Americans simply because they weren't Japanese. The Japanese were the overlords.

For a time Marcellus lived at his family place. The Americans were bombing Palau's airfield, which was near the family land, but starvation times had not yet come to Palau. Life was tolerable. When word came to Marcellus that his auntie in Melekeiok was sick, he went north to take care of her.

One afternoon in Melekeiok, Marcellus set off for an adjacent islet to collect coconuts. As the tide receded, it was possible to walk in shallow water the half-mile to the islet. Marcellus walked. He was twenty-one years old. He was young and strong and shirtless in the sunshine, and he carried a Palauan ax on his shoulder. He was the tall, central feature in that horizontal seascape. He knew that when he returned from the islet the tide would have withdrawn even farther, and he would be walking on dry sand; but right now, striding through the shallow water, the sensation was like walking on the surface of the sea. Marcellus was nearing the islet but was still some distance from it when an American plane appeared. There was no place to hide. The plane made a strafing pass, and Marcellus died.

No one is sure what happened to Singer's father, Kochi Koske.

"They shot him. No. He died of sickness," Singer Kochi says now, feeling he should say something. Obeketakl assumes that Koske died of starvation somewhere on Babeldaob Island. The last years of the war on Babeldaob were bitter. The Americans held Peleliu and Angaur to the south, and having no need for Babeldaob they left it alone. At first the Japanese officers, from fear of American planes, read their dispatches by the ghostly light of dried ostracods, held in the palm and moistened to trigger their luminescence. Later there were no dispatches. The Japanese took to the jungle, and with the Palauans lived off the land as best they could. Kochi Koske's grave, or bones, lie overgrown there somewhere. He was sometimes a timberjack, sometimes a charcoal maker, sometimes a brick maker. He was a gentle man, but very strong, his son has heard. Singer himself has no memory of his father. "He was a tall guy, a huge Japanese," Singer says today. "Six-foot two, two-hundred and twenty-five pounds." This could be so, but since it is exactly the size Kochi uses for all the big men in his life, it is probably more suggestive than precisely accurate. Koske was a big Japanese. It is interesting, though, that a man as large and strong as his son should need to remember a giant.

Singer's stepfather, Ngiraingas, was a good man. He was, and is still, a skillful spear maker and craftsman, a slight but strong-handed man with a bespectacled, scholarly, gentle face. He made spears well, but he was not good at throwing them, and throwing was what Singer wanted to know. Singer learned from a surviving older brother, Taro. Taro and Singer played hooky deep underwater, wearing homemade goggles and thrusting at reef fish with hand spears. Spearguns had not yet come to Palau. The two brothers played hooky standing in the eelgrass shallows at low tide, throwing their tridents at the fish that dart about there.

Learning to use a spear in eelgrass is nothing like learning to throw a football, which the boys of Koror Town were learning at this time from their first American teachers. Spearing is a football game in which your small receivers are trying to escape you, with eelgrass to hide behind and a three-dimensional field to dodge about in. A boy must learn to judge the depth the fish is moving at. His grip moves forward on the spear for deeper fish, an advanced grip giving his throw more power and a deeper angle. His grip moves back for needlefish and the other species that move near the surface and require a shallow angle. As the coordinates of the fish change, the spearman's hand dances up and down the shaft. A spearman does not throw simply at a fleeing fish, but at a part of him, and that part is different for the different species. For a bump-head parrotfish moving at a depth of five feet, for example, he aims ahead of the gills and a little above them. He tries to avoid hitting fish of any species in the gut, for fish are soft there and can wiggle free. Stationary fish are hardest to hit, oddly. Spearmen have trouble explaining exactly why, but they agree that the unmoving fish is usually the one you miss. Maybe the steady target makes the spearman lazy, or maybe a fish's motion in relation to various points of reference in the shallows helps correct for the distortion of the water.

Refinement of the spearman's skill takes a boyhood of practice. To excel a boy must love the idea of spearing. "I think I learned from willingness," Singer says today. The only time he cried as a boy was when they wouldn't let him go fishing. A good spearman is uncanny. He almost never misses. For a Western man who watches a subsistence spearman at work, there is a growing uneasiness in the wait for a miss. The subsistence art seems to violate all laws requiring a reasonable number of failures. You can't hit a home run every time—can you? The Western man wonders what principle keeps his own equations, or briefs, or couplets from being so unerringly on the mark.

Singer learned things that the boys in Koror Town did not. In those days, as now, Koror's streets and stores worked on Palauan boys like a sip of Lethe or a bite of the apple. Town boys liked to hunt and fish, and they were fair enough at it. Koror is not much of a town, after all, and its residents are not far removed from the ocean or the jungle. Yet where the boys of Koror might know how to find the holes of mangrove crabs, Singer knew, from the appearance of those holes, whether or not a crab was home. Hunting, he wasted no time on empty holes. He knew from the color and consistency of the muck sealing the holes whether the crab inside was molting. If the crab was molting Singer reached in and seized it, for its claws were soft and it could not hurt him. A Koror boy, unable to read such signs, thrust his spear indiscriminately into every sealed hole. If the crab inside was molting and soft, the spear tore it apart. A wasted crab or two did not matter, for the shelves of the corner store were lined with canned mackerel imported from Japan. It did matter to Singer, and because it mattered he could grope with assurance in the dark hole of a crab that in another season would have sheared off his fingers.

When Singer came to Koror Island to begin the fourth grade, he was a solitary Stone-Age boy. His new schoolyard was full of children. He had not known there were so many children in the world, and he was uncomfortable among them. He had spent all his previous life alone or in the company of his brother, perfecting his art with spear and net; he had not practiced any social arts. He could not understand the children's way of joking. The boy spearman saw only one course open to him; he became the terror of the school.

"The male heart is a stone," the Palauan proverb goes, and Singer's young male heart was stony. His warrior ancestors had fought with heavy wooden sword-clubs and slip-on knuckles studded with sharks' teeth, and Singer was faithful to that tradition. He was the roughest boy around. His Spartan youth on Babeldaob had given him all the tools he needed.

One day in art class when Singer was twelve, the boy behind him made a noise. The teacher, a young Palauan man, whirled and threw a piece of chalk at Singer, who from the teacher's vantage seemed to be the offender. The chalk exploded on Singer's forehead. Singer protested that he had not been the noisy one. Back talk was forbidden then, for discipline was still on a Japanese model. The teacher took up his rod and hit Singer on the head. Singer jumped up and pointed at the teacher.

"First you throw chalk at me and spoil my picture," he said. "Then, when I tell you it wasn't me, you hit me on the head with a stick. Now I'm going to kill you."

The teacher was too big for Singer to fight, so he ran home, got his fish spear, returned to school, flung the door open, and hurled the spear at the teacher. The teacher ducked and the spear missed. It pierced the blackboard and quivered there as the teacher ran from the classroom. The frightened man hid for a week, every day of which Singer hunted him—or so Singer says today. Finally the teacher slipped into Singer's house and begged Obeketakl to call her son off. When Singer came home, Obeketakl scolded him, and the manhunt ended.

In time Singer became a fair student. He drew and painted well. In the eighth grade, when Palauan students started learning English, Singer did well at that language, as his brother Marcellus had before him. "My name is Rukan. I live in a small island . . . " began the first English sentence he read. But Singer's heart remained stony. Like a gunman in one of the

American movies that were then showing at George's Theater, he was unable to go straight. By the time he finished intermediate school, he had speared or beaten a number of his fellow students.

Then, sponsored by an American employer who liked him, Singer went to Guam for high school. It was in Guam that he began to soften. The Guamanians are gentler than Palauans. "They didn't fight back, they just cried and ran away," he remembers. That quickly took all the pleasure out of fighting. The new code first puzzled Singer and then began to tell on him, but the outlaw in him died hard. If the natives of the place were friendly, there were other people to fight.

In those days the Guamanians were afraid of the black airmen from Anderson Air Force Base. Black Americans look very big and strong to most Pacific peoples. They did not look so tough, though, to the young men of Guam's small Palauan community. Palau is closer to Africa, by way of Melanesia, than any archipelago in Micronesia, and if the Palauans were not so tall as the Americans, they were just as black and strong. One night in a Guam restaurant, four black airmen pushed a Palauan around. The Palauan, outnumbered, left to seek out Singer and another Palauan hoodlum, and he found them. For Singer it was happy news. Singer and his two companions drove down to the beach in an old truck. They climbed several coconut palms, harvested the nuts and husked them. When they had a good number of mature, husked coconuts, all very hard and about the size of softballs, they dumped them in the back of the truck and drove to the restaurant. One black airman was standing outside. Singer walked up and asked the airman if he had wanted to fight a Palauan. Singer weighed 135 pounds then and was not very imposing. The airman did not take him seriously, and he told Singer to move along. Instead Singer punched the airman in the jaw with a rock he had concealed in his hand. The airman fell and shouted for help. His three friends ran from the restaurant, one carrying a two-by-four, one carrying a chair, and one empty-handed. Singer retreated to the truck, where his two Palauan friends waited with their coconuts.

The airmen had no way of knowing anything about Palauans. The accuracy of Palauan throwing arms has made deep impressions on peoples throughout Micronesia, but not beyond the islands. The airmen now ventured where Marshallese, Yapese, Trukese, and Ponapeans would have feared to tread. No amount of fighting knowledge gained in the streets of black America could have prepared them for husked coconuts.

The airmen did not know, for example, that Palauans grow up throwing stones. In Palau tiny boys shoot birds with pebbles fired from their tiny rifle arms. To play Frisbee with a Palauan boy of four, a Peace Corps Volunteer must explain first that the idea is to catch the thing. The boy's instinct is to stone it from the sky. Palau's conservation officer, John Singer Kochi, who is in ways still such a boy, has conceived the perfect Palauan trash can; its only opening would be a small hole in the center of a bulls-eye. In Palau young men sometimes settle disputes by throwing at rows of bottles. A common touch is to throw the last bottle in the air and break it in flight, like Wyatt Earp. If Palau ever has a movie industry, its duels will not be fought with guns, as in Westerns, or with swords as in Easterns, but with stones. The duels will be just as spectacular. A Palauan with a stone in his hand feels like David with his sling. Recently a visitor to Palau asked, "Is there any interest here in karate?" His Palauan host raised a puzzled eyebrow. "Why?" asked the Palauan. "Not as long as there are rocks along the roads."

But the airmen did not know any of this. They advanced toward the truck, and the Palauans cut them down like bottles.

Most of Singer's fighting was with Filipinos, for Guam's Filipinos shared the Palauan fondness for trouble. In the Palauan language Filipinos are called *Chad ra Oles*, "the Knife People." In Singer's time on Guam there were two Palauans there who had been paralyzed and disfigured by Filipino knives. The young Palauan men on Guam were wary of the knives, but undaunted by them.

One night in Agaña, a Palauan named Pedro got into an argument with a Filipino outside a restaurant. Pedro was new to Guam, and he was unsure of the customs there. He turned to Singer for advice. "This Filipino seems to want to fight," Pedro said in Palauan. "Is it all right if I hit him?" Singer said it was fine. Pedro hit the Filipino, who wavered, but stayed on his feet and walked away. The Palauans then entered the restaurant. As they were sitting down, Singer looked through the window and saw the Filipino walk to a parked jeep and take a knife from the glove compartment. Singer told Pedro about the knife and warned him to stay away from that Filipino.

Pedro, who was very drunk, nodded. The Filipino entered, approached the table and challenged Pedro to a fight. Pedro sensibly remained seated.

The Filipino was afraid to move any nearer to the Palauans' table. There was a standoff, and this did not agree with Singer. Feeling that the pace of the event was faltering, he told Pedro to pick up the glass ashtray on the table and eat it. (In Palau teeth are tools, and Palauan jaws are very strong. Today Singer uses his own slightly jagged set to open pop bottles.) Pedro, who was new to Guam and was still feeling his way, did as Singer suggested. Staring at the Filipino, he bit a chunk from the ashtray. It cut his mouth a little, but that evening Pedro was feeling no pain. The sight of a red-eyed Palauan staring at him, chewing glass, blood running down his chin, was too much for the Filipino. He turned on his heel and left.

One morning at George Washington High School, a Filipino boy, a friend of Singer's, opened a pocketknife and laid it on his desk. The teacher had not yet arrived. The Filipino announced to the class, but really to Singer, that in his opinion no sober man could cut a person. A man would have to be drunk, the boy said. To *cut* someone. To actually cut the flesh of another human being. It was impossible to be sober and do that. He turned to Singer, and asked if Singer thought he could pick up the knife and cut him. Singer kept his mouth shut, knowing that if he opened it to say anything, anything at all, those words would be followed by his picking up the knife and cutting his Filipino friend. The Filipino's theory about alcohol and violence was wrong. Singer could cut people cold sober. He was never anything but sober, in fact. He had not then, nor has he yet today, so much as sipped alcohol. The smell of it on someone's breath is enough to make him sick.

The Filipino mistook Singer's silence and persisted. He dared Singer to cut him. Singer demurred a second time.

"Like the eelgrass, he leans with the tide," Palauans say of an indecisive man. They call such a man "estuary water"—neither salt nor fresh—or to his face they say, "You are like the reef heron, who flies with legs dangling." Herons sometimes fly that way, as if uncertain whether to tuck their legs under them or stick them out behind. Many similar proverbs—in fact much of Palauan folk wisdom—attack vacillation. On the Filipino's third request, Singer picked up the knife and stabbed him in the stomach. Then he walked from the room.

The Guamanian students ran out behind him. They were all very upset and some were crying. The knife blade had been short, and the Filipino boy was not seriously hurt, but the stabbing had been ugly. The Guamanians asked Singer why he had done it. He had no answer for them. "When I pick up a knife, I can't just fake with it," he says today. "I have to use it. I don't know why. I have to go through with it."

In basic training in Hawaii, the sergeant showed Singer a red bucket.

"This bucket is white, isn't it, soldier?" the sergeant asked. Singer didn't get the idea. "No sergeant, the bucket is red," he said. The sergeant slapped his face, twice.

"Soldier, when I tell you the bucket is white, the bucket is white. Now what color is this bucket?"

"Sergeant, the bucket is white," said Singer.

Caught up in a strange system, in an alien land, Singer had been afraid to fight back. For the first time in his life he knew how it felt to be beaten and humiliated. It was a revelation. He had never lost a fight before and had never understood the pain he was dishing out. His former cruelty had been less a failure of heart than of imagination.

Singer was tricked into enlisting by a friend with a grudge against him. He thought he was just registering for the draft. In the army Singer began answering to his church name, John. His last name in those days, Ngiraingas, was unpronounceable by sergeants shouting roll. Instead they called him "N.G.," for the first two letters. He was now Private John S. N.G. and was in many ways a different man. But the S. still stood for Singer. The stoniness left his heart, but a straightforward spearman remained there.

One afternoon in Korea, where John played first base for his division's baseball team, it began to hail. John had never seen hail before. As the team ran to the shelter of the day room, John shouted, "Hey, it's snowing!" Everybody laughed. "Where are you from, man?" someone asked. Later that year, when real snow fell, John ran around with a peanut-butter jar and tried to catch it. Today when John tries to explain snow and hail to his Palauan colleagues at the biology lab, he has trouble. "Snow are different from hail," he says. "Hail are small and hard, like a marble. If they hit you it really hurts." Nina Dlutaoch, who listens from behind her typewriter, snorts at this—it's such an obvious lie. "Bulak!" she cries.

In Korea John's unit crossed frozen lakes and rivers. The soldiers had to put chains on the tires of the trucks. The notion of ice—of cold, rigid water—excited him and frightened him a little. John wore gloves and a cap that protected his ears. His breath froze on the fabric near his mouth, and the fabric became miraculously weighted with ice.

When winter was over, his unit moved up near the demilitarized zone. The land was barren. There were sandstorms. They made camp in that region one night, in the midst of desolate hills. In the morning hundreds of girls appeared there. Where had the girls come from? Private Ngiraingas wondered.

In Korea the smell of night soil was everywhere. The stink was the worst thing, after the fragrance of Micronesia.

In Korea the soldiers of his unit were warned to watch what they said in bars and hootches. There was no way to tell a North Korean from a South Korean, they were told. Anybody could be a spy. John was careful to remember this, and no military secrets passed his lips.

When his Korean tour was over, John was sent to Fort Benning, Georgia, where he volunteered for airborne. On his first jump over Georgia he was scared until the chute opened. "It seemed like I was going too fast," he remembers. "I felt like my intestines and everything was in my throat. But when the chute opened I really liked it." From then on he jumped as often as they let him.

One evening in Georgia, John and another Palauan soldier went with two white buddies to the theater. The other Palauan was darker than John and had nappy Melanesian hair. The ticket taker refused to let him in. "But he's not a Negro," John explained. "He's a Micronesian, like me. We're Palauans."

"I can't help it," the woman said. "He can't get in. Not with hair like that." The soldiers argued, but the woman was adamant. "Fuck it," said one of the white soldiers finally. "Let's go to the drive-in."

John is not sure why the woman approved of him. All Georgia smiled on him, usually. "I guess they thought I was a Mexican," he says. He simply noted the racism. One night he watched when a northern black soldier, having been refused service, tore the bar apart, but he felt no special vindication. He was more interested technically in how the black man went about busting the place up.

John had only three fights in the army. Trouble no longer attracted him. But when he did fight, he had the old advantage. There were too few Palauans in the army for them to have a reputation. ("Watch out for the who? The *Palauans*?") Palauans are not especially large or dangerous-looking people. American soldiers know nothing of the existence of men like Katusi, the Palauan who won the individual competition in the last Micro-Olympics. Katusi is a heavily muscled, black, ugly man from northern Babeldaob Island. In the coconut-husking contest, Katusi ignored the husking stake and tore his nuts apart with his bare hands. In the palm-climbing competition he ascended like an orthodox climber, but descended upside down. Palauans say that when Katusi feels there is not enough lime in his *chemeled*—the package of betel nut and lime wrapped in pepper leaf—he sprinkles more quicklime directly into his mouth. Not even his countrymen are certain that Katusi is human, but dress him in olive drab and he would look like any other soldier.

In his last fight John lost one stripe because his opponent was a master sergeant. The trouble started at the Fort Benning pool table over a game of six-ball. John had won forty dollars from the sergeant. John's best friend, a Mexican named Abiles, began taunting the sergeant about the money he was losing, until finally the sergeant pulled out a Japanese razor he had rigged with a push button and spring. He slashed at John, who jumped back. John must have been very quick at 140 pounds, for he is quick now at 200. (The razor laid his uniform open, he claims, though in this detail he may be making a good tale better.) The sergeant, after some maneuvering, backed him against the pool table. There was no place left to go. Keeping his eyes on the sergeant, John groped behind him and his fingers closed on the cool, hard smoothness of a billiard ball. At that instant the fight was over, though the sergeant had yet to learn it.

ONE WEEKEND John left Fort Benning and drove with some soldier friends to Saint Petersburg, Florida. Saint Petersburg was on the ocean, he discovered.

There were coastal mangroves there, and among the roots John saw what looked like the holes of mangrove crabs. With a C-ration of spaghetti, he baited a crab out and caught it. It was just like the mangrove crabs in Palau, but bigger. His Palauan crab knowledge proved less provincial and specialized than it might have seemed; it worked for him here, on the margins of another ocean.

John made a fish spear, fashioning its triple-pronged head from wire. He spent the day spearing fish. His friends were amazed by his skill and asked him how he learned it.

"I've always been spearing fish," he answered. "I've done this all my life."

⟿ 13

JOHN KOCHI steers into the morning sun. The white tropic ball has risen high enough that he need not stare into it, but the sea has spawned a thousand facsimiles, and all these reflected galaxies bounce their light at him. Kochi shades his eyes with his hand and frowns against the rays. He is fixed in a solar cross fire that can sicken a man of fair complexion in an hour, but Kochi is not fair. The sky is blue and nearly barren. Briefly a small cloud interposes, and for a moment the patrol boat moves in shadow. The moment rests like a mother's cool hand on forehead, checking progress of fever, but it lasts no longer than that. The sun peeks around the cloud, sees the boat again, and strikes with all its spherical weight.

At noon Kochi reaches his destination. He turns shoreward, steering for a grove of coconut palms. When the water is shallow enough, he jumps in and pulls the boat high on the white sand. Followed by his single passenger, he enters the palm forest. In the dappled, shifting shade of the palm fronds, the sandy soil is cool to the touch and inviting, but Kochi ignores his reprieve from the sun and sets to work. Shovel in hand, he stops at the first of several compost heaps. He digs in, then drops the shovel and sifts the earth through his fingers until he feels the thing he was hoping for. He grunts with satisfaction and holds up to the light the large, drab cocoon of *S. ruficornis*. The wasp is still doing well on this island, it seems. This cocoon is tombstone for one rhinoceros beetle larva. Kochi returns it to the compost heap. He infects the heap with beetle virus and moves quickly on. At the next heap he does not bother to search for cocoons, just mixes in the virus and moves again. When the job is finished Kochi lays down his shovel and walks off into the trees. A minute later he returns with two green drinking coconuts.

"Lunchtime!" he says. With three blows of his machete he lays a woody husk open, exposing the nut within, and with the point of the blade he carves out two drinking holes. He repeats this with the second coconut. "What'll you have, root beer or orange?" he asks his companion. The companion picks orange, and Kochi hands him the nut in his left hand. "Root beer for me," Kochi says with satisfaction.

He sits on the floor of the forest and raises his coconut to his lips. "Darkness into darkness!" he says, and drinks. This is a corruption, extempore, of a Palauan proverb. The proverb properly goes, "Like coconut juice, from darkness (within the nut) into darkness (within the stomach)," and it means, "Let's keep this a secret between us." Kochi is an open man, and the conventional application is of no use to him. He has turned it around and made a toast.

AFTER SOLDIERING in Hawaii, Korea, and Georgia, and a tour of duty in Germany, and army baseball in Japan, Kochi returned to Palau. Many of the Palauan men who undertake this sort of army odyssey become citizens of the outside world and find they can't go home again, but Kochi never doubted that he would return. Today he remembers his five years in foreign lands as if they happened in a movie. It is hard for him to believe he was really there.

On returning to Micronesia, he went to school at the Trust Territory Farm Institute in Ponape and then went to work in Palau's Agriculture Department. One day in the agriculture office he heard Robert Owen lecture on the need for conservation, and it made sense to him. He asked Owen for a conservation job, and he got it. Kochi's dedication to his new work was sudden, surprising perhaps, and total. Today the only effort required of Owen is to moderate Kochi's fervor, which sometimes gets out of hand. Owen has met no Palauan who feels conservation so deeply. There are Palauans better qualified educationally to take over Owen's job—one man now has a degree in marine biology. "But John is a natural naturalist," says Owen. "He has this complete missionary spirit. He's not perfect, but if I waited for someone who was perfect. . . ." Owen worries about the other claimants to his title. He worries, too, that Kochi will not live long enough to succeed him. Kochi has a recklessness that Owen has not been able to control. It almost would seem that Kochi has a death wish, if Kochi did not enjoy life so much. Kochi drives jeeps and boats too fast. He takes foolish chances with surf and reefs. His diving companions believe he gets "narked out" at one hundred fifty feet, the depth most of them accept as a safe limit, and they watch him closely down there, for he has a habit of suddenly heading straight downward. It is probable, though, that what his friends take for nitrogen narcosis is just a submarine manifestation of his strange fearlessness.

To become chief conservationist, Kochi will need a college degree, and soon he must leave Palau again to retrace the steps of his army odyssey, a prospect that both worries and excites him.

Kochi left Palau a lightweight and returned from the army a heavyweight. He carries his present 200 pounds easily, as if they were meant for him. His brothers Taro and Jimmy are slightly smaller but built the same; if John is a pocket battleship, they are pocket cruisers. The slender juvenile phase in the Kochi men would seem to bear no more resemblance to the adult than larva does to beetle. From certain angles the small man is visible in the large man, however. The Kochi shoulders are remarkably deep, but not so remarkably broad. The arms, for all their girth, are short.

Kochi is the long-ball hitter on Palau's baseball team. His ability to drive a ball for distance is a function of his weight and the quick wrists that have also made him Palau's Ping-Pong champion. Ping-Pong champion of Palau may not seem an impressive athletic title, but it is. Palau is an archipelago of athletes, and the competition there is rough. There are baseball minds in the Pacific who are convinced that Palau could field a team that would hold its own against Japanese professionals, and the Japanese have done very well lately against American teams. In Palau the boys grow up throwing stones and spears, and they develop very accurate arms. Every Palauan mother's table is a training table. The food is organic, planted or speared or trapped by the people who eat it. Spring-training weather lasts all year.

There was once a very good Air Force team from Guam called the Bombers. As part of a goodwill tour of Micronesia, the Bombers scheduled Palau, arriving very merry and so confident of victory that they bought a case of beer for the winners. You couldn't get much deeper into the bush league than the Palau Islands, the airmen thought. The Palauans beat them 23 to 0.

Palau's team is far better, Kochi believes, than any army team he played for. His army teams sometimes lost. In Korea his divisional team was bunted to death by a small, fast ROK army team—Private Ngiraingas decided they were called the "Rock Army" because they were so tough—who bewildered the American soldiers by throwing their bats at the ball. But nothing like that ever happens to Palau's team. Palau never loses.

It is interesting that the game Kochi remembers best was played not in Palau, but on Ponape, between the Trust Territory Farm Institute team, for which he played, and a team from the island of Kusaie. Kochi's stardom, among the lesser lights of what was truly a bush league, was brighter, and this, as much as the game's drama, made it memorable. Kusaie was leading until the final inning. The Kusaie pitcher, flawless through the first eight, became wild in the ninth and walked two men. Then he threw the fastball that Kochi drove over the taro patch that served as right-field fence. There were no automatic home runs on the Ponape field, but no one bothered to chase the ball if it reached the taro, and Kochi's ball had cleared it entirely.

It was Kochi's baseball reputation that first attracted his wife Ramona, a pretty, shy, sturdy woman from Angaur Island. Ramona Kochi is half-Japanese, like her husband, but she spends less time in the sun, has lighter skin, and looks more Japanese than he. Ramona has the easy grace of the barefoot queens who so impressed Von Kotzebue and other European explorers of the Pacific. A tooth missing at the corner of her mouth somehow makes her smile more charming. Kochi boasts about Ramona's toughness. As a girl she was a fighter, he claims. Ramona herself is modest about that, but it is likely true. Growing up in her village on Angaur, Ramona preferred the company of her brothers, and she liked to do the things boys did. She swam and fished with them, and she set traps for jungle fowl in the woods. In rainy weather, when the feathers of jungle fowl became wet and they couldn't fly, she chased them through the forest until they tired. She also learned gardening and cooking and the other female skills, picking them up by osmosis as all Palauan girls do, and she came to enjoy those things too.

As a young woman Ramona moved to Koror, where she went to work at Neco Store. John Kochi saw her there and asked her to a movie. She knew he was a baseball star and she liked that. They began to see a lot of one another.

One day when John was away at another island, Ramona's parents visited John's and discussed what a fine match their children would make. John returned to find that he was married. It was about time for marriage, he thought, and he liked Ramona, so he decided to give it a try. He went around to his girl friends' houses and collected all his clothes. Ramona took such good care of him that shortly afterward he took her to church for a Christian marriage, "to make it very affirmative."

Today everyone remains pleased with the arrangement. John considers himself remarkably lucky to have such a pretty and competent wife. "The woman is outrigger for the man," he says, quoting the Palauan proverb. Ramona considers herself lucky in having a good man who never beats her, as many Palauan husbands do, and Ramona's parents are so pleased with their son-in-law that when he is away, Ramona's life becomes very difficult. They are afraid that some other man will win her heart and they insist that she follow the old Palauan custom, leaving the house only when accompanied by one of John's relatives.

When her husband became conservation officer, Ramona was worried at first. The first fish dynamiter John arrested threatened to kill him. "What if they bomb us, John?" Ramona asked. "Don't worry," he answered, "if they do, it will just happen to them someday." This did not reassure her much, but the passage of time did, and today she no longer worries. She likes to go on patrol with her husband, and he likes her company, for he feels she brings him luck. He realizes that she is more patient than he. On two occasions when husband and wife were keeping a suspected poacher's boat under surveillance, waiting for their suspect to emerge from the forest,

Kochi wearied, but stayed a little longer at Ramona's insistence and eventually made his arrest. Ramona acts as her husband's agent, phoning the biology lab from the store to report that Mr. Ngirengelwangel or Mr. Bekebekmad has just bought a box of .22 shells, or to impart some other bit of intelligence. When Kochi begins to worry that he is too old for college—that maybe his brain has conked out on him—it is Ramona who reassures him. For Ramona, her husband's education in the United States will mean four years of separation from him and considerable hardship, but it will be best, she thinks, for her children and the future.

The Kochis have three daughters and a son. Their oldest daughter, Mabel, is four years old. She is afraid of Americans and hides whenever they come to the house. The younger Kochi daughters, Merci and Melanie, are too small to be afraid or to have much personality yet. They are very much like dozens of other tousled, naked, dark-eyed girls who play among their mothers' banana trees in the backyards of Koror. Kochi's son Stevie—Steven Singer—is six years old and is the pride of his father's heart. From the look of Stevie now, he will be stocky like his father. His skin is fair, but his father's was too, before winning its adult color in the sun. Stevie's hair grows Japanese-straight and sticks out all over his head like the spines of a sea urchin. His eyes are extraordinarily wide-set, large and black. Something in the way his attention ranges suggests a wolf boy—a human boy reared by wolves. When Stevie exits the house he leaves through the window.

Kochi has not taught his son to use a fish spear yet. He wants to wait until Stevie has learned to love the ocean and the idea of fishing, for he believes that a spearman's skill follows from that. He is afraid that now Stevie would just throw his spear at people.

EARLY SATURDAY MORNING, before first light, John Kochi leaves his house for the biology laboratory. He returns home just as the sun is rising, driving Number 35 Mitsubishi Diesel Jeep. He parks the jeep with the motor running and walks in his *zoris* across his grassy front yard, along a path worn down to the red soil. On Kochi's property, cassava fronts the dirt road, both mature plants and new-green plants just breaking the ground. His northern boundary is a row of banana trees, and behind the house is sugarcane

("*Saccharum officinarum*," he explains to any visitors). Ramona Kochi squats in her garden, working with a spade. She wears a pale-pink formal dress that is too old to wear formally. The sun has not yet struck any part of the yard, and the earth is still dewy and cool where she works. "Hey, quit working in the garden! It's too early!" shouts her husband, grinning, as he passes. She smiles absently, but scarcely glances at him. Her eyes are directed at what her hands are doing, either from shyness, or because she is preoccupied with some problem, or because her work requires it. Kochi steps out of his zoris and enters the house barefoot. The two rooms inside are small. The walls and roof are of corrugated metal, the doorway is doorless, and the windows are without glass. The plywood floors are clean and bare of furniture, except for an old Singer sewing machine that stands under one window. Stevie sleeps on the floor, wrapped loosely in a thin mattress. He looks accidentally entangled, like a lion cub who has begun by playing with the mattress, then has fallen asleep. In the warm Palauan night blankets are not necessary, and Stevie does without them. Melanie and Merci are awake, and they watch their father solemnly. Mabel is nowhere to be seen. Kochi walks to a tall closet where, to judge from the bareness of his floors, all his worldly possessions must be stored. He finds his badge and puts it in his pocket.

Palau's conservation badges were an idea of Kochi's. He saw a selection advertised in the catalog of a Honolulu company that specialized in law-enforcement equipment. The design he liked best was the one worn by the "Wisconsin marshals," as he remembers them. With his order for that style he sent a reproduction of the Trust Territory seal, to replace Wisconsin's, and the badges came back in the mail. Above the official palm of the Trust Territory runs Conservation Officer in bold letters. The number 1 badge belongs to Robert Owen. It embarrasses him a little, and it languishes in his desk drawer. The number 2 badge is Kochi's. The number 3 badge is intended for Kochi's assistant when there is money to hire one, but that has yet to happen. Kochi ordered these first three badges in gold and then seven more in silver—wild optimism, for today he remains a chief without a single Indian.

Kochi stands on his tiptoes and gropes on a high shelf for his gun. He finds it, a silver .38 police special with leather holster and cartridge belt.

Near the handle is the Trust Territory serial number, hand-engraved by someone who learned his calligraphy under the Japanese. Kochi walks to the jeep and stuffs the pistol in the glove compartment. It will remain there, unloaded, for the duration of this morning's patrol.

Kochi drives to the end of the Koror road and waits at the edge of the Babeldaob channel for the ferry. When the ferry arrives he greets the pilot and several other friends—he seems to know everyone aboard—and offers them his paper bag of betel nut. The Palauans begin the ritual that is the best part of chewing betel nut; the passing around of the bag, the peering deep inside to look for the missing ingredient. On Yap, where chewing is the national pastime and all jaws are robust from the constant excercise, this peering into betel-nut bag is the most common national posture. In Palau too it feels pleasant and sociable. Kochi and his friends each bite a green nut in half, thumb out some of the pulpy core, and sprinkle on powdered lime from a baby-food jar with holes punched in the lid. Each man tears off a fragment of pepper leaf, wraps it around the nut, and pops the package into his cheek. On Yap, pepper leaves are plentiful and the whole leaf is used, but in Palau the leaf is the scarcest of the betel-nut makings and is carefully conserved, for stingy use of resources is an old Palauan virtue. The men on the ferry chew and talk. The green betel nut reacts chemically with the white lime, turning their saliva red. Most chewers spit the first mouthful in a bright-red stream and swallow after that, but those with strong stomachs swallow the first mouthful. The effect of betel nut is mild. There is a flush—undetectable in darker Palauans—then a slight dizziness. The chewer's limbs feel cool and light. Sometimes he notices two damp, cool spots about the size of dimes on either cheekbone below his eyes. Palauans often chew betel nut when the sun is hot for the cooling effect, and students sometimes chew before a test, but for most people betel-nut chewing is just something to do, like smoking cigarettes.

Kochi wanders about the ferry, making conversation. He checks the luck of two fishermen who are trolling from the stern—if fishing from the Babeldaob ferry really can be called trolling. The ferry must be the slowest in the world, and sometimes a voyager is halfway across the channel before he realizes he is moving. Ferry trolling is more like fishing from a jetty that is drifting with its continent. The ferry crawls across on its two cables and deposits Kochi and his jeep on the Babeldaob shore. When he takes up the road again he is in Airai Municipality, his home district.

If *municipality* suggests city or town, then the word is misleading. An occasional corrugated-metal shack catches the sunlight in the green of the mangrove swamps and of the woods through which the road twists, and a few clearings are planted to taro and cassava, but there is nothing more municipal than this—nothing for the eye, at least. Yet municipality is an English word of which Palauans are very fond. It is almost as good as *principality* for sounding fine, and to Palauans it must convey a feeling for the former sovereignty of Airai, Aimeliik, Ngchesar, Ngetpang, Melekeiok, Ngiwal, Angaur, Peleliu, and all the other old autonomous districts of Palau.

When Kochi comes home to Airai his manner changes. He plays big shot, a bit. In Airai his clan has more prominence than in Koror, and here at home he is surer of his standing. Koror Town is a confusing place for more Palauans than Kochi. People from all of Palau's islands, municipalities, and clans have been drawn to Koror for the town's jobs, but they live there in uncertainty about caste. Most consider themselves expatriates and look forward to the day they can return home. Koror Town has existed for more than half a century, time enough, it would seem, for these difficulties to be resolved, but the town has yet to become a comfortable place. The ancient system and its allegiances are ingrained in the tissues of the people. Kochi has noted the change in himself when he crosses into Airai, and he is amused by it.

He stops now at a small store at the edge of his family land. He greets the proprietress, buys a Coke, and steps outside to drink it. The store's freezer has kept the Coke so cold that ice floats in it. He sips slowly in front of the store. He wants to be seen. He wants everyone to know that Singer is in Airai this Saturday. *"The conservation officer is here today!"* his presence shouts as he silently nurses his Coke.

"I hate to apprehend people," Kochi has said. For all his fierceness in pursuit of poachers, he does not enjoy catching them. His purpose is to stop poaching, not to make arrests, and he prefers preventive methods when they are possible. He travels about Palau continually, popping up at unexpected times and places, working hard to achieve ubiquity or a reputation for it. He wants every poacher to think of Singer when squeezing the trigger.

The sunny and serene palm tree on the badge in his pocket is not a bad symbol for his brand of justice.

Down the road from where the Conservation Officer prolongs his Coke, a small boy is throwing a fish spear at silver beer cans he has set by the roadside. In the ten minutes it takes Kochi to finish the Coke, the boy does not miss.

Kochi tosses his empty can in the trash and climbs into his jeep again. He drives north to the airfield, where Palau's only road runs out. He leaves the dirt of the road for the airfield's gravel. This Airai airfield is the nearest thing to a plain in Palau. After the shady windings of the woodland road, the airfield feels very open to the sky. The long runway is desolate on days when the plane is not coming. At one edge stand three shade shelters, with roofs of thatch on tall poles. From a distance the shelters look like the standards, or tripods, of a titanic army on an abandoned battlefield. This *was* once a battlefield, of sorts. The Americans preceded their invasion of Palau with a surprise attack on the airfield. The Japanese thought the approaching planes were their own and ran out onto the field waving flags.

Kochi accelerates until the jeep is doing fifty. In Micronesia the airfields are the only places where speeding is possible, and young Micronesian men like to drive there to see how it feels. The first traffic death in an archipelago invariably comes on its airfield, in a head-on collision between young drivers experimenting. As the end of the runway speeds closer, Kochi makes a joke about taking off and flying to Guam. For a moment it seems he really intends to do it. He has forgotten that he can't fly—a forgetfulness that comes on him often in motorized vehicles, both marine and terrestrial. The end of the runway races near. Beyond and below, the green savannahs and forests of Airai spread out magnificently, and the ocean sparkles in the sunlight. At the last instant Kochi swerves, brakes, and leaves the airfield on a red-earth jeep trail.

Bouncing through the savannah beyond the field, Kochi passes a ruined Japanese Zero. The rusty traces of the fighter plane are arranged around a perfectly preserved propeller. The propeller is the densest part of the Zero, and the plane leaves that, just as range animals leave their skulls. Kochi drives hard. Sometimes he hits a ditch too fast, and he and his seat rise several inches in the air. He has claimed he wants to wreck Number 35 Mitsubishi

Diesel Jeep so that the biology lab can get a new one. If he is really trying to wreck her, he is going about it like Penelope, for it is he who spends hours under number 35, keeping the jeep in what his maintenance reports call "a fairly running condition." When the jeep is feeling poorly, only Kochi can start her, through an amazing sequence of pumpings and adjustments. Today Kochi drives as if he wants to teach number 35 a lesson. He disdains the use of four-wheel drive, although the ruts in the road are pools of water, and the ridges between ruts are muddy and slippery. He prefers to stay unbogged by maintaining his momentum. He shifts to four-wheel drive only when he gets stuck. Finally he comes to a spot where the ruts have widened to ditches and are brimful of rainwater (in Palau it has always just rained recently), and for once he is admirably cautious. He puts number 35 in reverse and backs off to survey his problem. Then he jerks the jeep into gear and races wildly through. His caution was not admirable after all. His pause was only to anticipate which way he would slither.

The savannah that Kochi drives through is not natural. There was once forest here, but it burned away in fires set by Palauan arsonists. In Palau when forest is burned off, a tough, nearly immortal grass takes over, and the trees cannot return. Fires have been especially bad here on Babeldaob Island. A fisherman's-eye view of Babeldaob, landward from the reef, reveals the great length of the island as a patchwork of dark-green forest and new-green savannah. The island must have looked very fine in the old days, when its twenty-five miles of forest ran dark and unbroken from southern tip to northern.

The fires have hurt the lagoon as well. Burned-over country does not hold soil as well as climax vegetation, and in places the runoff from burned land has muddied the extraordinary clarity of Palau's lagoon waters and injured the coral communities that depend on that clarity. The fires are the worst conservation problem in the Palau Islands.

Pyromania is a strange aberration anywhere, but in Palau it is especially strange. Here, as in the other small islands of Micronesia, the traditional view is that land, in its scarcity, is precious. The people have never been under the illusion that their terrain is anything but a life raft. On an island, people cannot abuse their acres and then move on, for there are no more acres to move on to. Alienation of land in Micronesia is difficult, as the United States government has discovered in trying to acquire a little for its military purposes. Within such a tradition, then, arson seems a peculiarly mindless and self-flagellatory behavior, like that observed sometimes in caged animals. It is hard to believe that arson would have been tolerated in the days when the messengers of the chiefs enforced kerreomel. If it does not hint at something dark and unhinged in the new Palauan psyche, the widespread occurrence of the fires does at least suggest that, after a century of foreign rule, the old systems are breaking down.

John Kochi is both gentler and more leery in his view of arsonists than of poachers. He recognizes something sick in the former. For the latter there is profit in breaking the law, and Kochi has no sympathy.

From time to time Kochi stops and turns off the engine. He listens for gunshots. There are none. He leans back in his seat and lights a cigarette. There is no sound in the savannah but the birds. He smokes and listens to their music.

Part
Three

14

THE RUINS of the Japanese epoch are abundant in Palau. Many Palauans remember Japanese times fondly and look upon these ruins sadly. Under the Japanese there was more happening in Palau. There was a buzz, an excitement, and a promise of more to come. Palau, everyone said, was to become the Japanese Riviera. If Palauans could vote on it, some say, a majority would pick the Japanese over the Americans. These Palauans forgot the bad things about Japanese rule—that Palauans were second-class citizens, beaten occasionally, conscripted for labor at the whim of the government—or perhaps they remember all that, but feel it was a fair price for the affluence the Japanese brought.

Koror Town was a city of twenty thousand in Japanese times. It was a model-scale city. There were narrow paved streets where Japanese sailors strolled in the innocent, little-boy sailor suits of the time. A few of the broader streets were lined with stately palms, in the shadows of which they seemed avenues. The residence of the High Commissioner for the Japanese South Pacific was more elegant than anything the Americans have built in their own occupation. A broad stone staircase led up to the commissioner's door, and a carved wooden balcony in the Japanese colonial style ran entirely around the second story.

Today only vestiges of this modest grandeur remain. Near the Koror village of Ngermid there is a miniature pagoda that once housed a lantern and marked the entrance to a temple. The temple is no longer there. It was leveled by bulldozers, as were most Japanese buildings that survived the bombing, on the orders of a bitter American general who, the story goes, had lost a son elsewhere in the Pacific. In the heart of Koror Town, looking fiercely down on a dirt street, are two imperial lions of stone, guarding the gateway to nothing.

Relics of the fighting between America and Japan are everywhere in Palau. They are so common on Koror Island, which was Japanese headquarters, that they lose their poignancy. But on other islands, where the monuments to war are scattered and overgrown, to stumble upon them is to feel their ghosts.

On Babeldaob, hidden in the labyrinthine convolutions of that island's jungly coast, is the entrance to War Cave. The cave is called that because, in the old days, war parties from Koror assembled in it before advancing farther. Much later, during the American siege, the Japanese used the cave as a salt factory. By night the besieged Japanese quietly rowed far out from land, to where the salt water of the lagoon was not diluted by the freshwater runoff, and there they filled their barrels. Back inside the caves, where the fires could not be seen, they boiled off the water in troughs cut from fifty-gallon drums. Because the cave ran deep into the porous limestone of the island, splitting into numerous caverns, the smoke could dissipate within. No tendril ever found its way out to give the salt makers away. Today the apparatus rusts on the cave floor.

Before becoming conservation officer, John Kochi led tours to the cave. Few tourists came to Palau, but when they did it wasn't a bad way to make a little money. Kochi would stop first at Yap Money Cave, where the Yapese people, Palau's nearest neighbors, quarried the great round stones they used for currency. There was no suitable stone in Yap. The rareness of the stone, and the risk in obtaining it, was what made it valuable. When Kochi's tourists had their fill of the stones, he would cross the channel to Babeldaob and pause offshore over a Japanese seaplane that looms greenly there under thirty feet of water. He would visit War Cave last.

War Cave is not very impressive, aside from its history, Rusted salt-boiling troughs lie about, The squeak of bats sounds from among the stalactites of the ceiling, but a tourist can't see any bats. Kochi decided that the cave needed more color, and for one tour he persuaded several boys to dress as warriors and hide in the darkness. As the first tourist, a lady, entered the cave, the boys ran at her yelling. "That lady, she took off," Kochi says. "She was an old lady, but boy could she run. 'Hey!' she says to me, 'things is still very primitive around here.' "

On Arakabesang Island, adjacent to Koror, the Japanese had a seaplane base. The base has been reclaimed almost entirely by greenness. Its field is so broken by clumps of returning vegetation that it is difficult to grasp how the place was laid out. One taxiing area is discernible and several ramps running down into the water. There are a few craters from American bombs, but not many. The Americans did not feel threatened by the field, for when their invasion troops landed there were no more Japanese planes left. In the spots that are free of vegetation, the field's white cement is still perfectly flat. The cement was poured in great squares, and the sides of these are still rectilinear. At the edge of the largest open spot, in the shade of the encroaching woodland, several Palauan families have built houses, and one house stands out on the cement itself. This seems a strange site, hard and uncompromising ground to have chosen. The unshaded house is assembled of corrugated metal and cast-off lumber. It stands on pilings in the dazzling plain of squares, surreal and apocalyptic. It looks like a dwelling built by survivors from the salvage of a ruined civilization, and that is, of course, precisely what it is.

One day recently an old Palauan net-fished for sardines where one of the seaplane ramps angles under the lagoon. The fisherman waded in knee-deep water, watching for the surface disturbances that mark schools of sardines when they change direction. The fisherman selected a school and walked over to intercept it. He shuffled his knees forward gently in a way that did not disturb the water. His outrigger paddling canoe followed behind, fastened by a cord to his belt. The cord left his hands free for the throwing. As the school shifted toward him, he cocked himself, dropping his right shoulder and bringing both hands back to his left hip. For a moment he waited, with the peasant patience that lasts out empires. Then he uncoiled, and the weighted net flew out. His follow-through left him with his right hand extended toward the school. Beyond his fingertips the net formed a perfect circle in the air. It fell flat on the water, and its weighted circumference sank instantly. The fisherman waited a moment. Then he pulled on the net line, drawing the net toward him. At the same time he gave his canoe line a tug; the canoe jumped forward and caught up from behind. The fisherman lifted the net, its bottom heavy with squirming silver fish, and he emptied it into the canoe. He picked out those sardines caught in the mesh and he tossed them in after their fellows. He gathered up his net again and resumed his wading.

ON KOROR ISLAND, near the causeway to Malakal Island, lie the ruins of the Palao Tropical Biological Station. The station was a simple place, and it has fallen to ruins that are not impressive. The committee of Japanese scientists who ran the Palao station had to rely on the charity of the island's businessmen, so they had money only for necessities. The only elegance was a pair of stone stelae that marked the entrance. The laboratory was a frame building with large windows of leaded panes. When the station's scientists, sitting at the seaward window on the laboratory's hard wooden stools, looked up from their microscopes to rest their eyes, or looked up from the row of weighing balances along the workbench, they saw, through the leaves of the banana trees outside, the blue water of the channel and the islands of Malakal and Arakabesang beyond. From beneath their window a path ran down to the little jetty and the mangroves of the Koror shore. To the right of the path, coral specimens lay drying in the sun. When the scientists swiveled their stools they could look out the landward window at the green of Koror Island rising behind them.

The laboratory apparatus was old-fashioned. In the past thirty years, lab equipment has changed a lot, and Japanese marine biology in the years before the war was even then behind the times. Old photos of the Palao laboratory, with its wooden stools and heavy brass microscopes, look much like the photographs of Charles Darwin's study in Kent, though not so plush. The row of balances, graduated in size, seems the work of craftsmen and not machines. There was more brass in everything. The brass microscopes probably did not magnify so well, but they appear to have been more satisfying to look through.

At the center of the room was a large cement sink with spigots for seawater and fresh. The sink had a wooden deck with spaces between planks so that the working surface could drain. There were always rows of bottles and beakers drying there. The laboratory was equipped with a hand centrifuge, a Minot microtome, a paraffin oven, a Van Slyke gas apparatus, a Kipps gas generator, a water distiller, a compound microscope, alcohol lamps, and several dissecting microscopes. Workers were reminded before they came that if they needed more specialized equipment, they should bring their own. The price of alcohol was low, workers were told, five gallons for five yen.

Near the laboratory was the coral-specimen-exhibiting shanty, a small building three by four *ken* in area. Except for a small darkroom of one by two ken in the southeast corner, the entire shanty was devoted to the exhibition of coral. When necessary the shanty was used as a guest room. There was also a large boat with a three-horsepower kerosene-oil engine, and a small rowboat with oars and sailing gear.

In its early days the station had no library, and of all the shortcomings this caused the most anguish. "The problem is financial, but deplorable nonetheless," the director wrote. Workers were advised to bring their own reference books. "We had felt endless loneliness in the limited bibliography before establishment of the library," wrote a biologist named Genji Kato. Kato conceded, however, that the limited bibliography "gave us encouragement to some extent. We enjoyed reading after hard study under sunshine of the Tropics, receiving cool wind blowing through leaves of trees." But it was a great relief to everyone when the library was finally established.

Prospective workers were screened by the committee of scientists. Personal character, health, and academic career were thoroughly investigated. Among the scientists who passed muster were Fujio Hiro, who came to Palau to do fundamental research on animals symbiotic with reef corals; Noboru Abe, who studied coral distribution; Motoki Eguchi, classification of corals; Hiroshi Enami, influence of hormones on the change of chromatophores. The Palao station was interested in corals almost exclusively. Corals were where the money was—it was a coral-reef fund that paid the way of the scientists to the islands. Some of the Japanese work was good, in the opinion of Robert Owen, who runs Palau's present biology laboratory, and some was very poor. Owen believes that the postwar research of the scientists he has invited to Palau is generally better.

In their monographs the Japanese were even more careless than Americans at rendering Palauan names. The American *Babeldaob* is much closer to the Palauan sound than the Japanese *Baberdaobu*, and the American *Peleliu* is much closer than *Periryu*. The Japanese in their prefaces never acknowledged the help of Palauans. One would never know from reading the monographs that the Palaus were islands with indigenes. But the Japanese scientists were very generous in acknowledging previous papers by Americans. The Japanese seem to have looked to America for leadership in marine science. And each Japanese preface glowingly acknowledges the Palao station's Japanese director. (Today American scientists seem to prefer acknowledging Palauans to their own colleagues or countrymen.) The Japanese scientists were satisfied with very little. They worked for the love of science alone. Only their travel to Palau and living expenses there were paid.

The war was an annoyance to the scientists at the Palao station. The war effort diverted funds that might have been used for research. The director's house, built at a cost of twenty-five thousand yen solicited from Japanese companies in Palau, was the pride of everyone at the station, but belonged to the director for only six months before the military appropriated it. The scientists accepted such inconveniences with good humor. They were under no illusion that their annoyance mattered. They did not think much about how the war might change their lives. They worked on happily among Palau's bright corals. The war seemed very distant to them even as it swung very near.

The director of the Palao station was Shinkishi Hatai, of Tohoku Imperial University. Like Robert Owen, Hatai was engaged in a survey of the Pacific when he first came to Palau. Like Owen, he "particularly admired the richness of the fauna." Like Owen, he recommended Koror as the site for a research station, and like Owen, he found himself in charge of it. Like Owen, he loved the place and did not want to leave.

It would be impossible today for these similarities to escape Owen. On Owen's shelf at the biology laboratory is a set of Hatai's reports, and Owen has read them. Owen receives letters intended for Hatai. As late as

1967 one of these ghost letters, addressed to "Monsieur le Directeur, Tropical Biological Station, Palao," was delivered to Owen's lab, asking Hatai-Owen for information on Palau's marine isopods. Owen routinely answered it. And whenever Owen drives to Malakal Harbor, he must pass the ruins of Hatai's Palao station laboratory. The ruins below the road are not very apparent from above, but Owen knows what lies overgrown there. Shinkishi Hatai did not leave much of a monument. Owen's life story has had a dry run in Palau, and the first version did not end happily.

Today all that remains of the Palao station's buildings is the gray cement of the foundation. The coral-display shanty, or what seems to have been the shanty, is now a square of earth enclosed by low foundation walls. The square has been planted to taro. The owner of the surrounding taro garden simply stepped in over the wall and continued her planting, and the rows of her young taro plants march as if the foundation did not exist. The low wall of the Palao laboratory is used by the woman of a nearby house to dry her bright-blue rug. On cleaning days the rug drapes the wall like cape over barrera in the sun. The station's round water tank, its roof collapsed and its interior open to the sky, is now a great vase full of giant, long-stemmed orange flowers. The banana trees have multiplied. Two large mango trees have grown up and spread their dark-green foliage to block what was once the view, through the laboratory's leaded glass, of the channel waters.

The Malakal channel, an arm of the body of water the Japanese called Iwayama Wan, "Rock Mountain Bay," is as blue as ever, though, and Malakal Island rises just as mountainous and green.

Shortly before the war struck Palau, the Japanese scientists packed up the station. Their departure was hurried, and they were not sure where they would settle again. The Celebes would be a good site for a new station, they thought, or perhaps certain islands off New Guinea in the Banda Sea.

"We long for unknown things," wrote Genji Kato. "In this meaning the Banda Area is a unique position for us to investigate the Tropical Science. We expect satisfaction of our advance into the Tropical Science by this area. We are endeavouring to realize it, feeling boundless joy and pride to have opportunity of playing a part. Those who were pursuing for brighter light in the South may be able to work actively under the equator.

"Now the materials and instruments of the station were totally sent to Macassar and all of the buildings of it were subscribed to the Micronesian Government. The laboratories were entirely cleared off. The floor seemed for me very broad. I looked round laboratories, director's official house and investigators' lodgings. All were vacant, as everything transferrable was sent to Macassar, packed in 402 boxes, which were all the station gathered during these 10 years. I left there with a mute bow, when it was 6 A.M., June 12, 1943, just before the hot sunshine began to gleam brightly."

FROM THE PALAU BIOLOGY LABORATORY:

A Selection of Drawings

by Takesi Suzuki

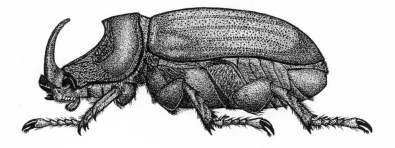

Oryctes rhinoceros
(coconut
rhinoceros beetle)
Palauan: *mengalius*

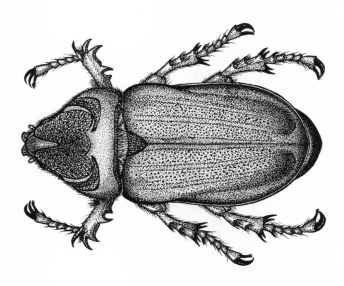

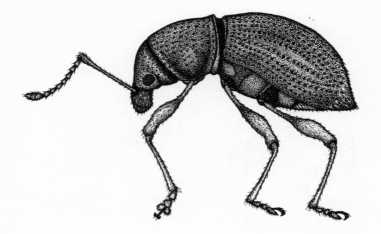

Trigonops ——

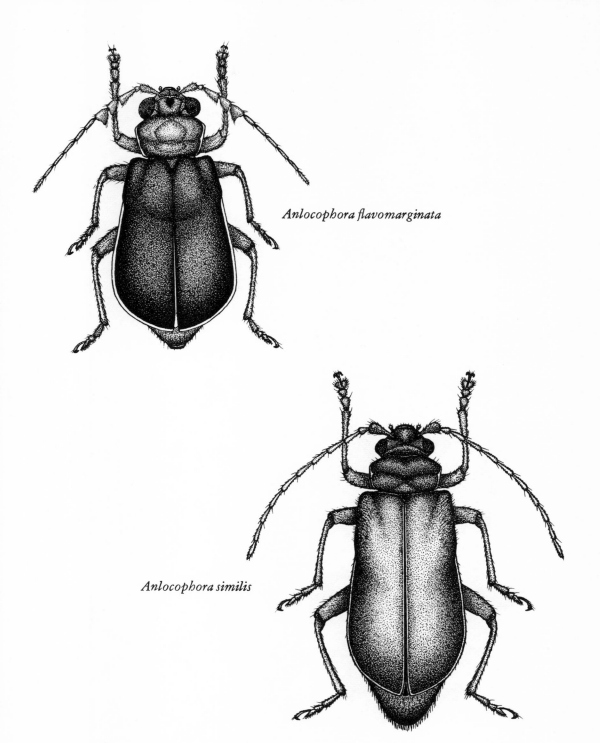

Anlocophora flavomarginata

Anlocophora similis

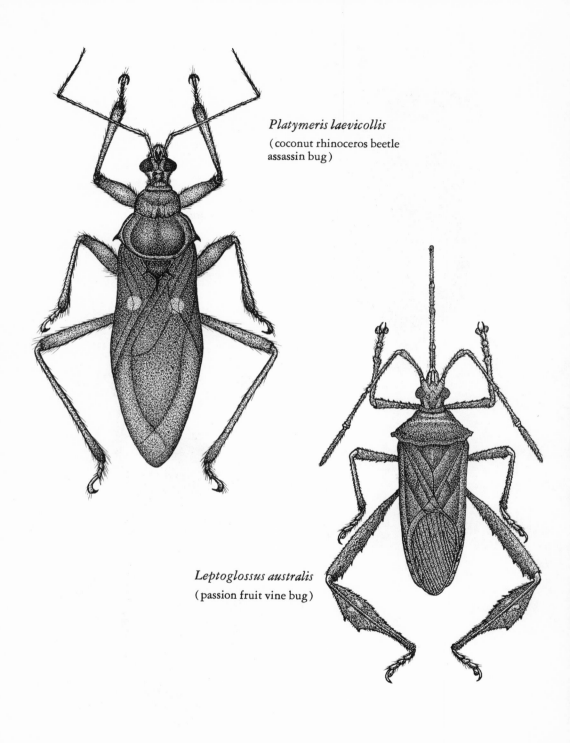

Platymeris laevicollis
(coconut rhinoceros beetle
assassin bug)

Leptoglossus australis
(passion fruit vine bug)

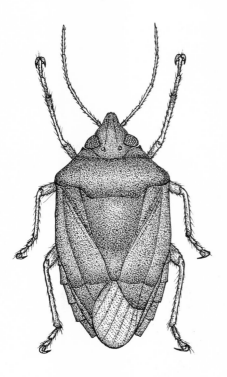

Nezara viridula
(southern green stink bug)

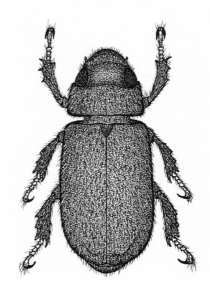

Adoretus sinicus
(Chinese rose beetle)

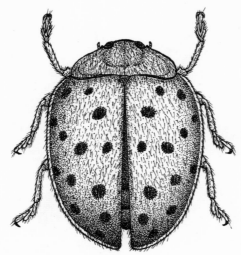

Epilachna philippinesis

Caroliniella anescens

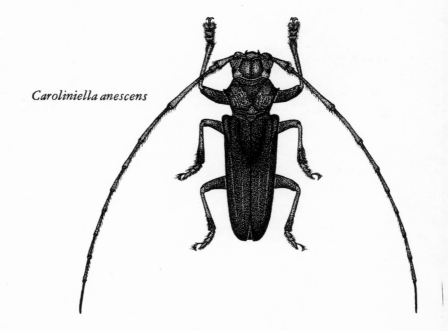

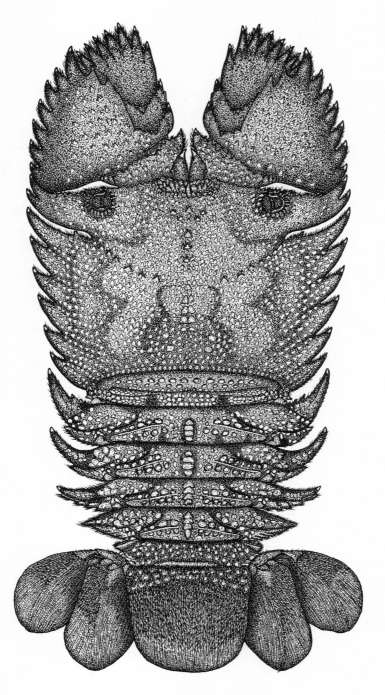

Syelarides neocaledonicus
(slipper lobster)—Palauan: *braber*

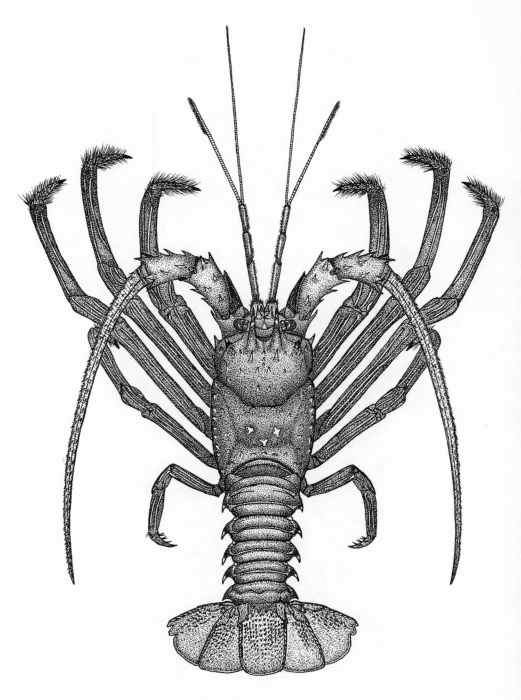

Panulirus penicillatus
Palauan: *raiklius*

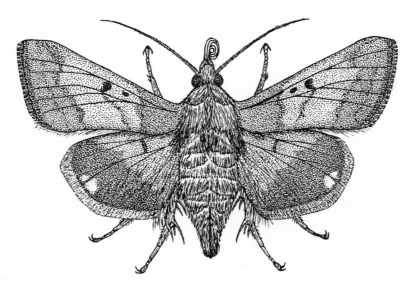

Heliothis zea
(corn ear-worm)

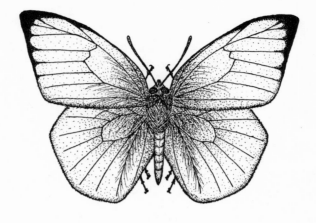

Captosillia pomona

Delius

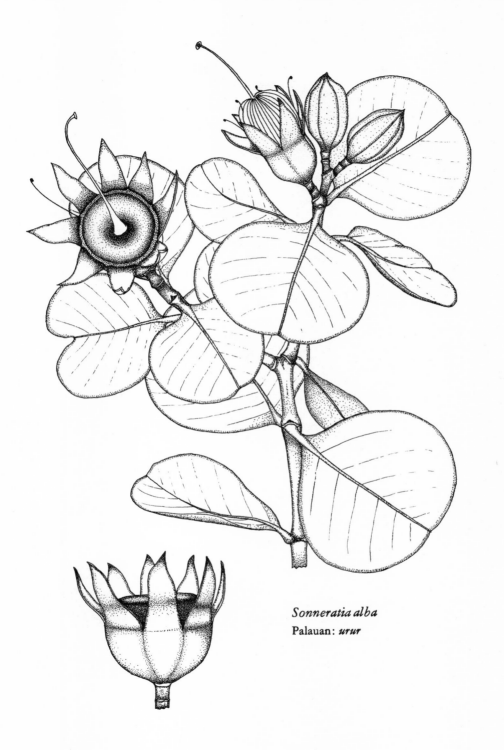

Sonneratia alba
Palauan: *urur*

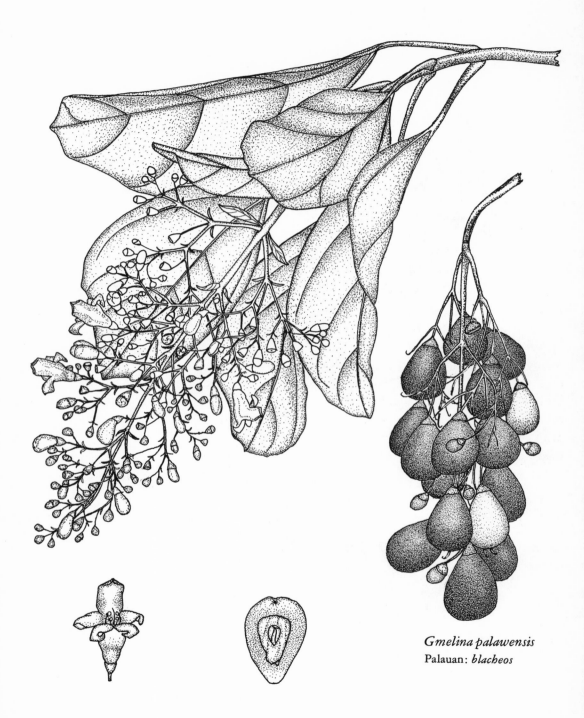

Gmelina palawensis
Palauan: *blacheos*

~15

ROBERT OWEN sits in his living room and speaks of his friend Bert Bronson. He chooses his words carefully. Between sips of scotch he sets his glass on the coffee table and slouches back in the sofa. The night breeze comes balmy through his window screens, carrying snatches of Palauan conversation and occasional exclamations by children and dogs from the shacks below the hilltop. Owen's coffee table is a plank cut from a piece of driftwood riddled with teredo holes. On the wall behind him are Douglas Faulkner prints, in color, of corals and fish, and Takesi Suzuki drawings, in black and white, of plants and insects. Owen gazes out the window, remembering things about Bronson and glancing from time to time at his listener.

"Bert came to Hawaii in the thirties," Owen says. "He had spent one year in college in Oregon. He didn't like it. He was a non-Establishment man. At first in Hawaii he was a beach bum, and that's when he got interested in sea diving. Then he learned a trade. He was a reefer mechanic. He worked on ships during the war. After the war he came to Guam and worked for the navy. But he spent all his spare time in the water, spearfishing and diving. There was a lot more life in the Guam water, then.

"Bert was a born naturalist. He was very knowledgeable, but not educated in a formal way. He became regarded as an expert, quoted in scientific journals and so forth. He was very knowledgeable about shells. It was Bert who got me interested in marine biology. He came to Palau when he could, and I went up to Guam. We spent all our time in the water.

"He quit his mechanic job and opened a shell shop. I sent him his first batch of shells. It was before I realized how very bad shelling is for the reef. The shop was real junky. He'd have fakes around, and little signs. He might offer a shell for seventy-five dollars, a very common shell that wasn't worth anything. If someone offered to buy, he wouldn't take them up on it. He had a nice aquarium in connection with the shop. It had a small shark with a remora attached. An octopus. Live cones. He charged ten cents to see it.

"The shop was in a building on the water. Bert owned the whole thing—he called it the Micronesia building. There were several shops besides the shell shop. There was an insurance office. A jewelry shop. I forget what else. A bar called the Pink Elephant. It was a good property. If Bert had run it right, he would have been almost wealthy. But he had no business sense at all. When people were really interested in shells, Bert would just give them away. One time I was talking to him in the store when some customers came in. Bert's back was to the door. 'Bert, you've got customers,' I told him. 'Sssh,' he said, 'maybe they'll go away.'

"Bert was coming around to conservation when he died. It was one of the things that bothered him about the shop. 'Look Bob, I love the ocean, and here I'm helping to destroy it.' Bert would rave and rant about the profit system. About advertising, and the legal system. He was a terrible businessman. His genius was for living."

Owen breaks off and goes to look for a photograph of Bronson. He enters his small study and rummages around. Two Rajah Brooke butterflies, framed and behind glass, decorate his study bookcase. Among the books are *Crocodile Hunt, Sexual Life of the Savages, Primitive Art, The Caroline Islands, Origin of Species, The Year of the Whale, Tropical Planting and Gardening, Useful Plants of Guam, Philippine Orchids, The Naturalist on the Amazon. The Pagan Tribes of Borneo, The Beauty of Women, I Learned About Women from Them, Women of all Nations.* There is some Melville and Conrad, but otherwise little fiction. On an adjacent wall are engravings, one entitled "*Abba Thulle, King of Pelew, together with Ludee, his wife & Prince Lee Boo, their Son.* Another is *View of the Causeway, or*

Landing Place &c. near Pelew the capital of the Pelew Islands. It was engraved by someone named Wilkes, from a sketch "Drawn on the Spot, by an Officer of the Antelope Packet." Owen finds the Bronson photograph and returns with it to the living room.

In the photograph Bronson sits in swimming trunks, facing the camera. He looks tough and strong. His hairline is receding. His arms are powerful, his chest and shoulders hairy.

"When he and I and Sid Seid were out together, we looked like a group of apes," says Owen, who is a hairy man himself. "Bert hated to wear shirts. He almost never wore one. Periodically he shaved his body. I don't know why. Maybe he thought it made him easier in the water. I don't know. Maybe he expected to meet a mermaid.

"Women liked him. He was pretty marked up, though. A sea wasp had left a hole in his back. A shark, or it was a moray eel, I think, had scarred up his leg. A stonefish put him in the hospital for several weeks. Part of his thumb was eaten away where he had touched the stonefish. He said it was the worst thing that ever happened to him. His trouble with morphine was a result of the pain from the stonefish, he claimed, but Bert was embarrassed by his problems and he found these excuses.

"He was an alcoholic. He had undergone some kind of cure, but now and again he would fall off the wagon. When he fell off, it was in a big way. I've seen him drink half a fifth of gin without stopping. He would go on a binge until he put himself in the hospital. He was head of Alcoholics Anonymous in Guam, so he had to do most of his drinking around the house. He could handle the alcohol, I suppose, but somewhere along the line he ran into other things, and that's what killed him.

"There were always Micronesian students staying with him. Haruo Adelbai, who works for me now, was one. The house was always full of natives. Bert and Elizabeth adopted one Micronesian girl—she's sixteen now, a beautiful girl—and then they adopted a Palauan girl friend of this daughter. One time a guy was pestering one of the girls staying with him, and Bert got mad. He had this war club from Truk or Ponape. He was a gentle man, but this kid broke into the house and tried to rape the girl, so Burt chased him with the war club and sent him to the hospital.

"He was a great reader. We had discussions about everything. We agreed, shortly before he died, for him to come down to Palau for a few weeks and let me talk to him on the tape recorder. Just the kind of conversations we'd been having, but they would be there on tape.

"He was very funny, too, a practical joker. He was always putting up those crazy signs in the shop, the signs about rare shells that weren't rare. And he was a con artist. He could twist people around his finger to get these things he thought he needed, but that he didn't need.

"He spent two years in prison. He killed a man. It was very strange. Bert came in one day from the ocean. He stopped by the bar, the Pink Elephant, and was talking with the bar owner about business. He was sitting at a table with a friend of his named Olson. He wasn't drinking. He was in his swimming trunks still, with his underwater knife on his leg. There was a drunk at the bar who started to make cracks. The owner told the drunk to shut up, but the guy kept at it. Bert drew his knife and slammed the butt on the table. The noise scared Olson, apparently, because he jumped up, and tripped, and fell on the table. The knife went in his stomach and entered his heart. He died instantly.

"The trial was a political thing. The same week a Filipino had stabbed his wife to death. On the very face of it, it was the same crime. There was talk of discrimination in the courts against the Filipino, though in his case the stabbing was intentional. They both got the same sentence—two years.

"Bert had so many friends trying to get him out of prison. A biologist named Smith arranged to take him out on the water every day. They were making a fish collection. Smith was so impressed by Bert that he dedicated his book to him."

Behind Owen as he speaks is a portrait of himself. The portrait hangs modestly low on the wall, between two Douglas Faulkner prints, one of an orange skunk clownfish looking out from a pale meadow of anemone tentacles, the other of red sea whips. The portrait is by an acquaintance of Owen, Williamson Mayo, an American painter with a Palauan wife. The portrait is slightly larger than life. The greens and blues of Palauan daytime are reflected in Owen's face. The Owen of the portrait might be explaining his friend Bronson. The painted moment catches him glancing sidelong at a listener—eyes villainous or vulnerable?—to see if the listener understands. But this evening, beneath the painting the real, life-size Owen gazes straight ahead. He is saying that Bronson's death had not surprised him. There were, he says, a number of things that prepared him for it.

"He was possibly the best friend I ever had, but toward the end—I hate to think about it now—I began to avoid him. It made me so sad. And I knew he wanted me around and needed me. But what do you do when one of your friends goes down the drain?

"I wanted him to move to Palau. I thought that might straighten him out. Palau is the best diving in the world, you know. If I had moved him here, I would have helped myself too. The times we were together he was in better condition than when we weren't. I never drank when I was around him. I don't know what he would have done for a living here. He had the property in Guam. His wife could have handled the business. In fact, every time he was laid up, business would pick up.

"He was buried at sea. I couldn't get up there; it happened too quick. But I sent a letter that they read at the burial."

Owen never thought to ask Bronson what was wrong. They were not men who shared that sort of thing. Owen has no idea what was at the root of his friend's troubles. He sips his scotch now and tries to think. "He was non-Establishment," Owen says finally. "Not in a political way—more like a hippie. He was unable to adjust to modern life."

Hera Owen joins her husband on the sofa.

"Bert was instinctive in the water," Hera says. "He was as natural as any animal in the sea. He knew exactly what the cowries were doing, in tune with the tides and the time of year. At full moon we would go with him to get crabs. He would go singing Tahitian and Tuamotuan songs. He had lived in those places. Guam was the end of many travels for him."

"He spent thirty hours a week in the water," says Owen. "I don't know how his skin took it. 'This is a real good time to be out,' he would always say. I remember watching some small coral fish with him once. 'Want to see one up close?' he asked me. He snapped a fish in the back with a quick motion and caught it up in his hand and showed it to me.

"He's the one who got me going strong on marine biology. It was his enthusiasm, and knowledge, and the fascinating stories he had to tell about the animals. He was especially observant of marine behavior. Fish, corals, everything. Parrotfish, for example. Parrotfish feed on coral, and the ichthyologists used to figure, I think, that they just munch away at coral heads, digest the living parts, and void the skeleton. But from observation of parrotfish for hours and hours, Bert deduced, and suggested, that they must have some mechanism in the mouth or gills for separating the living animal from the exoskeleton, passing the inorganic matter out through the gills, and voiding only digested animal matter. The experts laughed, but later it was proved true.

"Bert discovered a four-inch marine shell that lives buried in soft coral. I think it may have been a new species. At least, certainly, no one knew it lived in Guam before. He had many, many first records of shells for Guam. He described their habits too, which is something few collectors do.

"In Micronesia there's a little commensal fish, called a pearlfish, that lives its adult life in the rectum of a sea cucumber. Every once in a while it ventures forth. Bert made observations on them. He had the patience to wait for the pearlfish to show up."

Earlier in the evening Owen said that Bronson was possibly his best friend. He must have been thinking about that, for now, suddenly and firmly, he restates it. Perhaps the scotch is bringing out the truth.

"I'll tell you how much I liked the guy," Owen says. "I liked him so much, I think I'm going to see him again."

He is silent for a moment and then speaks, trying to sum Bronson up.

"Mostly he just liked to lie out in the ocean and look at things. He spent *days* on end doing that. We'd go out in an outrigger or a bamboo raft, and we'd just take some taro. You know? Or we might fill that out with some fish. Bert would eat lying on the raft.

" 'Well Bob, let's go home,' he'd say, and he'd just roll off the raft into the ocean."

OWEN IS NOT quite ready for dinner. He speaks briefly of office affairs—Bronson seems to be off his mind—and then he begins talking of magic. Hera gently urges him to the table. Apparently she sees the signs that they will be eating a cold dinner.

"Someone in my organization has been using magic like mad against me," Owen says. "It's having an effect in the office. My people don't know which way to go."

Owen mentions the name of the man using the magic, a long-time employee who thinks that with Owen gone the way will be cleared for his rise to power. Owen is fond of the man and is clearly hurt about his resorting to magic.

"They see us making ten times the money they make. Unless they do a lot of thinking, they get a screwed-up attitude. Magic is the one way they can think of to equalize things. So when somebody gets after me too hard, I'll go out and get the other kind. Countermagic. Like I did for Maguadog. But for Maguadog it was too late.

"I've come considerably away from inflexibility on the subject. I'm pretty sure that it works in the minds of the people who believe it. But I think my belief is a little more than that. I don't know how much more.

"Even anthropologists who make a business of it can't jump the gap. As Kipling said, east is east and west is west. Until we get so mixed up it doesn't matter any more. They have magic and we have magic. Mine might be psychology. We have witches and they have witches. Which witch is which?

"Science has destroyed some superstitions, but as far as I'm concerned, it's just made a dent. The curve of science will make some turns and twists but will come out parallel. Science will never solve all these things. No matter how many millions of years. As soon as we don't have an unknown, we'll all explode. To less than atoms. You've got to have a mystery. And the people in religion have solved it much better than science, for now. Because scientists have blown up a few myths, they think they've got them on the run. But it's so infinitesimally small.

"Before this is all over," says Owen, rising for dinner at last, "I'd like to investigate the soul of the sea cucumber. If I've got one, they've got one.

"Where do all the good sea cucumbers go?" he asks. He is headed for the kitchen to refill his glass. He pauses at the kitchen threshold, smiles, and answers himself. "They go to some place where pearlfish can tickle them. We all like these basic things, huh?"

~16

"THIS IS the best chicken I ever ate," John Kochi has a habit of saying, or ". . . the best *sashimi* I ever had," or ". . . the best sunrise I ever saw." He will probably make the same claim for tomorrow's sunrise, but that is not to say he doesn't mean it today. The days of Kochi's life get progressively better. Tomorrow's sunrise *will* be the best. When the latest best thing is sudden and full of drama—like a very big shark—Kochi lets out a long, whispery, intense "goddamn!"

Kochi does not seem to be much of an aesthetician. He does not seem to see the subleties of green when he looks at vegetation, but botanical detail and the problem of identification.

"Look at those clouds, man! It's going to be a good sunset," he often says, or words very similar. He seems really to be saying, "It's going to be a *big* sunset." His pleasure in the sunset is like his pleasure in catching a big fish.

Kochi sees and hears things before other people.

Once he sat on the beach of one of Palau's remotest islands, watching the sunset and talking with a scientist he had been guiding. "Frigate birds," Kochi said, and he pointed to a red cloud near the horizon. The scientist saw nothing and he doubted that Kochi did either. He knew Kochi well and he was familiar with Kochi's tendency to exaggerate. Then he pointed his telescopic camera lens at the patch of sky that Kochi had indicated. He

158

saw the birds. Even when magnified, they were difficult to make out. The scientist was studying their flight when Kochi pointed overhead. A frigate bird was passing above them, a dot against the sky. "Ha!" laughed Kochi. "Look at him cleaning himself!" The scientist stared at Kochi in disbelief. He could scarcely make out the bird; yet Kochi saw it preening.

All the rest of Kochi's senses are uncannily acute. It seems possible, sometimes, that his interest in the natural world is less temperamental than physiological. He can't help but love the life around him, for it comes home to him so clearly and vibrantly. Kochi turned again to the scientist. "That's the best sunset I ever saw," he said.

"As if I were pregnant, I am full of life," goes a line from a Palauan chant. Kochi's own joy in life is ex utero, not quite containable, and it takes forms that are not Palauan. In a society where modesty is a great virtue, Kochi is boastful, moderately so among his countrymen, it's true, but often wildly so among his American friends. The boastfulness is a way of venting the joy. Kochi's claims for himself are usually about 125 percent true. His baseball statistics, as he recites them, have not been included here from a suspicion that in print they would embarrass everyone.

In the lab office one day Nina Dlutaoch was telling Kochi of a man she knew with balls so tough you could kick him between the legs and it wouldn't faze him a bit, when Kochi interrupted to say that he had tough balls too. A baseball hit him there once, he claimed, and he just kept on playing. Having said so, he immediately looked doubtful, but he let it stand. If it was not exactly true, it should have been; his balls felt tough in spirit. Kochi's habit of reciting scientific names, too, seems more than anything else an expression of his joy in life. It is an un-Palauan habit, and probably un-American as well. "*Terminalia catappa!*" he greets the tropical almond. "*Artocarpus communis!*" he salutes the breadfruit. "*Areca catechu!*" the betel-nut palm. "*Intsia bijuga!*" the dort tree. "*Semecarpus venenosa!*" the poison tree, for Kochi bears no grudges. "*Casuarina equisetifolia!*" the iron-wood. Kochi's pleasure in the names seems a little insane. It is as if he imagines there is magical power in the knowledge of the names, as there once was in simply knowing the names of the Pacific gods. Demei Otobed, Kochi's friend and colleague, shares this name mania, and the laboratory conversations between the two brown men sound like those of ancient Romans.

Kochi's pleasure in science goes deeper than the names. He has a vast capacity for absorbing scientific fact when it is imparted orally. He serves as guide for the scientists whom Robert Owen invites to Palau, and he forgets little of what they tell him. When a scientist talks, Kochi watches the man's face as if it were a fish he is about to transfix with his spear. The only field of natural science in which he is largely in the dark is geology, for few geologists come here. In matters of science Kochi's boastfulness leaves him, for some reason. If he does not know the Latin for a plant, he says so, after a sad pause.

Kochi's desire for knowledge of a thing is too closely tied to his acquaintance with it—plant or animal, cloud or current—to be called academic. For all his Latin, he would not be happy as a Linnaeus, describing pressed or bottled specimens from someplace else. His science is not so very different from a fisherman's or a hunter's lore, and not so un-Palauan as it might seem. Science is just something extra that Kochi has. Subsistence spearmen like himself, in living close to the life around them, have a knowledge truer than science. Kochi's imitation of the sound a dugong makes when it has risen to breathe, for example, goes straight to the essence of the animal's nature. Dugongs are great, homely, vegetarian sea mammals that have found one of their last refuges in Palau. Even here, they are few. One reliable and observant old fisherman-chief estimates that in all his years, he has sighted them on only seventy occasions. They have been as rare to this man's lifetime as summer solstices. In the daytime the dugongs float, dozing, out on the lagoon, diving whenever a boat approaches. At night they come to shallow water to feed, and it is then from certain places that one hears them in the dark. When Kochi imitates their sighing inspiration—it is a nearly human sound in his mouth—he somehow conveys all the creatures's rareness, all its gratitude for the sweet night air and for life itself.

"Ah," says Kochi on another day, speaking for himself, not dugongs, wearing his number 28 Asahi football jersey and sipping coffee from a mug labeled John K. at his desk in the lab office, as a tropical rainstorm drums on the metal roof above. "There's nothing like coffee on a rainy morning!"

ANCHORED IN THE NIGHT, twenty yards from a black line of reef rocks, an empty boat tosses gently on the lagoon. Seaward, in the direction the prow points, a dark rim of clouds lies on the horizon, and above the line of cloud the sky is full of stars. In the other direction, to the stern, the long, low silhouette of Babeldaob Island and the silhouettes of Koror and the elabaob islands have merged with darkness into a single mainland. Only the position of Koror is certain, for above that island the lights of town illuminate a low cloud—a false moonrise. The ocean is calm and murmurs against the barrier of the reef. The air is still warm. The boat would be very solitary, here under the huge heaven of stars, at the edge of a lightless ocean, except that nearby two light beams move underwater. The lights are greenish and friendly and brave in the blackness of the water. They show as slender beams when searching at angles to the boat, and as pools of light when pointing in the boat's direction. At long intervals the beams are obliterated for the briefest of instants by a very bright white flash. The flash radiates like heat lightning but elapses sooner, ending too quickly to tell how far it traveled. For an instant it seems to have illuminated the entire ocean. Someone has just taken an underwater photograph.

The lights swim toward the boat and become flashlights in the hands of two divers. The divers pass underneath, inhuman in their face masks and fins, looking about with a terrible intelligence, painting the floor of the lagoon with beams of light. As they draw away again, their laboring fins hide their heads, and the intelligence seems not so terrible after all, just shocking and alien in this element. Long bubbles roll from the divers' mouths, separate into tiny bubbles, and jiggle upward. At first the bubbles, responding to the stress of that lower world, are cylindrical, and each tumbles up on its long axis. They become rounder briefly, then flatten as they near the surface. At the very last they are dome-shaped like the bells of jellyfish. They break the surface around the boat and jump out of existence.

The divers who emit the bubbles are only remotely like divers in motion pictures. The ocean they move in is limitless. Their bubbles do not rise vertically, as a movie screen in its narrowness implies, but with latitude and sweep. The ocean is uncontained and alive not just in its corals and fish and plankton, but in itself, in its shift and surge. For someone new to it, the living embrace of the night ocean is full of a nameless terror, but neither of these divers is new. They search the lagoon floor in a businesslike way.

The two disappear behind a jumble of coral heads, and all sense of scale departs with them. The coral heads might now be battlements. The searching lights are now just a glow that rises, subsides, and rises again, like fires within an undersea city burning greenly. Then the divers reappear above the battlements, which quickly become coral heads again, and they swim toward the boat. Rising for the side, they are dorsoventrally flattened by the distortion of the water and they do not look at all like men. First their noses, and in a moment their eyes are visible behind the glass of the masks. The beams of their flashlights shift from green to yellow, and then, in the last submerged instant, to white. As the flashlights break the surface, they lose their underwater auras and their mystery. John Kochi returns to the atmosphere first, followed by Douglas Faulkner, an American whom some consider the best underwater photographer in the world. Each man pushes his mask to the top of his head and seizes a rung of the boat's rope ladder. When Faulkner has finished all the wheezings and spittings of a man just returned from fifty feet, he says wetly, "Geez, wasn't that disappointing?"

"Nothing," agrees Kochi, "no fish."

The divers pull themselves over and into the boat, and they unharness their tanks. Faulkner towels off his camera and changes film. Kochi lights a cigarette. As they sit debating whether to dive again, the wind comes up. Without their having noticed it, the dark rim of cloud on the horizon has advanced to fill most of the sky, and soon not a star is visible. The boat, which earlier had been tossing on the swell, now begins rocking. The divers have trouble reading one another's face. Faulkner has extra trouble, for Kochi is so dark. They know each other well, however, and they reach an unspoken agreement not to dive again. Then they speak, agreeing to wait out the rain and waves and to begin the homeward passage when the tide is higher and the lagoon calmer.

The waves roll over the barrier reef without breaking, but the line of coral rocks excites the ocean's phosphorescence, and points of light dance along the line. As the divers watch, a denser, brighter constellation of phosphorus appears in the lagoon and moves seaward against the march of waves. The two men debate whether the constellation marks wave action or a living creature. Kochi argues for creature. Faulkner shines his light at the phosphorescence finally, to end the dispute. In the circle of light a surprised sea turtle turns its head toward them. Faulkner's flashlight has worked like a reverse X-ray, putting flesh on the turtle's foundation of electrons. With a single thrust of its flipper the turtle disappears.

It begins to rain.

The divers are weary, and the rain further dampens their spirits. Earlier today they were very noisy. Loading the boat at Koror in the afternoon, the two men, realizing that they would soon be on the water, could scarcely contain themselves. The prospect was too much for them. They laughed wildly at terrible jokes or at nothing at all. Douglas Faulkner, like Kochi, is in his mid-thirties, very fit and strong, and he shares Kochi's boyish satisfaction with things. Faulkner likes to get naked in the boat, lie on the bow, and stare at the waves as they speed at him, inches from his face. He stares as if the ocean rewarded persistence and will soon reveal some secret to him. Earlier this evening, when Kochi pointed out the best sunset he ever saw, Faulkner looked up dutifully, but quickly returned to his staring. Kochi did not mind. The Conservation Officer had no human company, so he spoke with the birds, cupping his hand to his mouth and calling to terns when they passed over. Sometimes a tern would swing toward the boat, and Kochi pretended his tern call was the reason. Then Faulkner broke out of his spell and the two men resumed joking. Kochi's boastfulness grew in leaps and bounds, and Faulkner listened with a smile. Kochi is usually careful with his language, but in Faulkner's company he curses freely. Palauans call this kind of talk *tekoi el kerekei*, "words of the lagoon," for in the heat of chase on the lagoon, Palauan fishermen are allowed to use rougher language than on land.

Kochi and Faulkner have a running joke about decompressing. Whenever one of them needs to relieve himself in any way, he uses this metaphor, and neither man ever seems to tire of it. "Excuse me while I decompress," Kochi says, unzipping his fly, and Faulkner grins as if it were an original line. But now, in the darkness and rain, they are silent. Both men wear long-sleeved shirts underwater for protection against hydroids and stinging corals, and the rain plasters their shirttails against them. They huddle to wait out the weather.

Waiting is contrary to the natures of both men. When the rain slackens somewhat, Kochi starts the outboard. He announces that the tide is high now over the inner reefs—an odd announcement, for minutes ago he said it was low. Faulkner seems to find no inconsistency there. He directs Kochi into position above the anchor and yanks it up. The boat starts homeward, bucking oncoming seas. Every fourth or fifth sea sprays the occupants. The water is warmer than the air, and the warmth lingers for several moments before the cold wind drives it away. For someone whose seas have been temperate, the idea of warm waves is unacceptable, even after countless sprayings, and every fourth or fifth sea breaks as a pleasant surprise. Neither Kochi nor Faulkner is new to the tropical ocean, however, and for them this warmth is as it should be.

The spray brings phosphorescent plankton aboard. A spark lands on Faulkner's arm, and he flicks it away instinctively. It is easy to forget that plankton light is heatless, and Faulkner has forgotten. A spark alights on Kochi's elbow. He lets it burn there coldly. Soon Kochi has stars at elbow and knee, then in his hair. From Faulkner's vantage, Kochi's darkened head and shoulders are framed by the boat's luminescent wake. The fan of the wake is fixed in shape, but new plankton is continually igniting and racing through it, blurring the edges of the fan, making it tremulous and ghostly. Faulkner peers hard into Kochi's face, but catches no glint from teeth or eyes. He can't make out a single feature. In the set of Kochi's heavy head and shoulders, there is no clue to his mood. Kochi sits darkly at the center of the milky wake, like a faceless cosmic king on a throne of starlight.

Now and then Kochi slows suddenly. A wave pattern, or a reference point in land, or an unaided recollection, has told him that a shallow reef is near. Twice he makes a sounding with a bamboo pole, discovers that he has several feet of water, and yanks the pole up. "Wow! It's deep, man!" he says happily both times. When the last of the fringing reefs is behind him, he twists the throttle up full speed, and the boat speeds homeward.

THE NEXT EVENING, dusk finds Kochi and Faulkner far to the south, above a submerged reef off Ngemelis Island. This reef at Ngemelis has an underwater cliff that is unusually beautiful, and a part of it is so fine that Faulkner and Kochi keep its location secret. "John, this isn't the place," Faulkner says when Kochi has finished casting about for it. "Yes it is," Kochi assures him. "This is the place, Doug." Faulkner defers to Kochi's judgment in these matters. He throws out the anchor.

While there is still light in the sky, the divers snorkel about, getting the lay of the subterrain. It remains surprisingly bright underwater when the sun is just down. Floating prone, the snorkelers drift inches above the plateau of the reef, looking down through their face masks at the small gaudy fish that peek up from alleys and archways in the coral. It is a various and densely populated country. Then, with a stroke of a fin, the razor's edge of the cliff passes beneath, and the plateau drops away into a blue void. Someone new to diving, finding himself suspended above the drop-off for the first time, sees the blue as sinister, full of the things that might come out of it. The Ngemelis cliff is notorious for its aggressive sharks, and the novice's imagination tries to materialize the light blue of shark in the deep blue of the void. But neither Kochi nor Faulkner is new to diving, and this blue potential of shark holds no terror for them. Kochi, who claims to fear nothing in the sea but large groupers and crocodiles, once gave a brief bit of instruction to a novice:

"Don't panic underwater. If you panic, you're finished. Be brave! *Sharks?* Shit."

The novice waited for more advice, but none was forthcoming.

On an earlier trip to this same cliff, Kochi's job was to stand at Faulkner's back and fend off sharks, allowing the photographer to give his full attention to the wall of coral. Faulkner turned from his viewfinder occasionally to check on the progress of Kochi's battle, and grinned around his regulator mouthpiece when he saw that his defender had made a game of fencing with the sharks.

The snorkelers return to the boat for dinner. Faulkner's wife has filled a basket with Japanese noodles, chicken, and bamboo shoots. The two men dip in and eat with their hands. Faulkner drinks a can of Pom apple juice, a Japanese brand, and Kochi drinks a Coke, finishing it off in three swallows. He tells Faulkner that the chicken is the best he ever tasted. The dusk deepens into a fine warm night with a crescent moon. Behind the boat looms Ngemelis Island, heightened now by darkness. A soft and rhythmic *crump* of waves sounds from the shore. The fragrance of land comes and goes with the changes of the wind.

The divers return to the water, this time with air tanks. Their flashlights shine again underwater. The searching beams are of about the magnitude of the stars above, but the light is greener, not so cold and pure. From time to time Faulkner's camera flashes from beneath the cliff. The flash seems to travel forever seaward, but landward it is terminated by the hard, black line of the reef's edge. The brightness lingers on the retina of the memory, so that in successive dives, as Faulkner works along the cliff, he maps it with light. The mind's-eye, time-lapse cliff shows as long and surprisingly straight.

When the divers run out of film or air, they return to the boat, seize the gunwale, let their regulators drop from their mouths, and hold a brief conversation.

After one dive Kochi spits out his regulator as if desperate for air and asks a question explosive with impatience. Clearly it has been on his tongue for some time.

"What are those things? I never see them before in my life."

"Sea pens, I think," Faulkner answers.

"Sea fans?"

"No, *pens*." Faulkner spells it out.

"Oh," says Kochi, glad to know the name.

After another dive, Faulkner rises first. The regulator has scarcely fallen from his mouth before he is asking, "Wasn't that tube coral beautiful? Geez that was lovely!" Kochi is too busy becoming an air-breathing animal again, coughing and spitting, to answer right away. Faulkner, full of the loveliness of the coral, has not noticed his friend's dilemma, and he persists. "Wasn't it lovely?" he repeats, looking intently at Kochi beside him in the water. Kochi smiles and answers yes when he is able. He really means it.

As the night wears on, the divers begin to tire, and after one dive Faulkner rises irritated.

"John, you've got to light those corals from the side. Not from behind like that. The way you did with the tube coral was perfect. But when you get behind me the flash attachment blocks the light and I can't focus."

"I know it, Doug. But I have my speargun in one hand and my flashlight in my other, and I got a problem."

"You do have a problem. I know it." Faulkner is sorry he spoke sharply.

"I'm going to leave my speargun next time," says Kochi conciliatorily.

Diving again, they pass a ledge where a basket star spreads its white plumes in the darkness. In photographing the basket star they discover a difficulty: it begins to fold up as soon as Kochi shines the big flashlight on it. When they have an opportunity to talk, they devise a strategy. Kochi will wait until Faulkner is in position, then hit the star with the light for the moment it takes Faulkner to focus, then cut the light after the flash of Faulkner's bulb. On subsequent dives they hit the basket star going and coming. Between dives they laugh about the star's dilemma, but they are sorry too for their repeated one-two punch of flashlight and bulb; they are weary themselves and they sympathize.

Changing film, Faulkner follows the rules of an old personal ritual without deviation, despite his fatigue. First he towels himself off, so that no water will drop from him. Then he towels off his camera. He opens the watertight case and runs a corner of the towel around the gasket, on the remote chance that the seal has leaked slightly. He straightens his back in the middle of the operation and groans, then bends again to his task. The boat's Coleman lantern has run out of fuel, so Faulkner works, and Kochi watches, in the glow of a flashlight lying on the seat. Lit dimly from below, the faces of both men are deeply etched by shadows. They look dead tired, satanic.

Faulkner likes to push himself. He believes that no photographer works harder underwater. He is proud of the number of rolls he has shot by a given date and is obsessed with the number he has yet to shoot. He sets goals for each day's diving. Kochi understands this kind of thing perfectly. Once when Kochi lived in Guam he went spearfishing for twenty-four hours straight. He wanted a lot of fish to sell so he could buy a car, and having started, he did not want to stop. Now he reminds Faulkner that tonight's goal is seven rolls.

"One more roll here," Kochi says, "then we'll go to the shallow place and shoot the last roll."

Faulkner looks at him bleakly. Being pushed is a new sensation for Faulkner, and is both pleasant and annoying. He is a competitive man, and his discovery of someone who can match his endurance underwater has not been entirely happy. Kochi makes him a little edgy in another way. "Nobody watches me photograph as closely as John does," Faulkner has said. "He knows exactly how I work. One day I gave him an underwater Nikkonex and a roll of film, and he was gone. I didn't see him again. He was off working for himself. He got some good stuff on the roll."

So Faulkner smiles now, in spite of himself. He nods, agreeing to Kochi's plan for spending the last two rolls. They saddle up, swinging their heavy tanks to their backs and buckling their belts. Each takes a short series of experimental puffs on his regulator, a series unique to each diver, like fingerprints. They tumble backward over the side, Faulkner holding his camera against his chest to protect it from the slap of the water. They float to a prone position, kick, and glide off like phantoms over the coral plateau. They don't hesitate at the edge of the cliff but plunge over. They kick down against what seems, in its resistance, a dark current rising from the bottom, and they disappear into it. Their bubbles can't follow. The bubbles sensibly abandon ship and raft in the correct direction, upward.

When the final frame of the seventh roll has been shot, the divers raise anchor and head for a nearby elabaob island to pass the night. They plan to return to Koror in the morning, when floating logs and other dangers are visible. The island has a sheltered cove and seventy yards of white-sand beach. Under the pandanus trees that line the beach, there are sandy places fine for beds, and there are potential beds of casuarina needles under the casuarinas. The beds require only long pants for a mattress and folded towel for a pillow. But the divers choose not to use them. Either because they are sea people and feel more comfortable on the water, or because each man wants to show the other how tough he is, they anchor twenty yards from the beach and make the best of the boat's cramped seat slats.

They talk for a while. From the unused beds on shore, their sleepy voices are audible, but it is impossible to make out the words. The conversation falters. There is the sound of someone decompressing into the water and then silence.

With dawn's earliest light, a bird calls in the steep forest behind the beach. The morning bird sounds like a sleepy and slightly blue child blowing experimentally on a flute—long, listless notes. Out on the boat the conversation resumes and continues lazily for a long time. Then Kochi's shape rises bulkily and he poles the boat shoreward. The prow grinds to rest on the sand. Kochi jumps out, crosses the beach, and disappears into the forest, leaving a line of tracks in the sand. The toes of each pair of tracks points outward. He reappears shortly, returning from whatever mission he had in the trees, and jogs across the sand, jumps in the boat, and poles out to where the water is deep enough to start the outboard.

Neither diver looks well rested. They both look like hell, in fact. Faulkner's eyes, he tells Kochi, feel like twin decompression holes in the snow. But both men are gay and ready for the day.

Kochi sets his forearm across the steering wheel, rests his forehead against it, and peers out from beneath its shelter at the morning glare on the water. Faulkner lies on the bow and stares down at the waves racing under him. Halfway home, Kochi surrenders the wheel and begins to set his boat in order. He discovers, in moving the air tanks about, that his final tank of last night's dive has considerably more air left than Faulkner's. He pauses. It seems to take him a moment to decide how to play this. Could a fuller tank mean something unheroic in the capacity of his own lungs? Or does it suggest a better breathing technique? He decides there is a strong case for the latter.

"Gee, Doug, I have a lot more air left than you," he says.

Faulkner looks briefly back at Kochi and the tanks.

"Remember, John, you're just holding the flashlight when we're underwater," Faulkner says. "That doesn't require much oxygen. I'm constantly moving around to get the picture."

Later, back at the biology lab, someone asks Kochi if the trip tired him. "No," Kochi answers. "I'm never tired on the ocean. I think I am born to be a man from the sea."

~17

ROBERT OWEN'S THOUGHTS turn often to a number of small, landlocked salt lakes in the elabaob islands. To Owen's mind the lakes are reversals of Darwin's Galápagos. They are islands of water shut off from one another by seas of land, and each lake in its isolation has undergone a separate evolution. "The fish in the lakes, even the common species, look different from the ones out in the lagoon," Owen says. "They're larger, or smaller, or have a slightly different color." There is enough biology in the lakes for several lifetimes of study. When Owen retires, or earlier if his work for the Trust Territory allows him time for pure science, he wants to investigate the lakes. If the work proves both promising and too much for him alone, he will apply for a grant and get help.

Palau's salt lakes resemble crater lakes in that their containing walls are roughly circular and slope steeply inward, but the encircling stone is not volcanic; it is limestone, the work of ancient coral polyps, whose old reefs have been raised above the sea and are now densely forested. Through tunnels in this coral rock, the lakes connect with the lagoon outside. Like forbidden chambers in a story by Scheherazade, each lake holds a different surprise. The pattern is for a single species to dominate each.

Salinity will prove to be an influence on the population of a given lake, Owen suspects, but more important will be the size of its connections with, and its nearness to, the sea. The size of most of the connections is unknown, but most seem to be small, for the tides in the lakes are sometimes six hours off the tides in the lagoon. Some of the lakes may be fed by filtration through the limestone, and into these lakes only the smallest larval forms will have infiltrated. Owen expects to discover new species in the lakes—the lakes have existed for thousands of years, long enough for species differentiation—but more valuable will be discoveries on associations of plants and invertebrates. The lakes that Owen has visited personally are more than sufficiently interesting to justify research, he is convinced, but what of the lakes no one has visited? What creatures, and associations, and discoveries wait in those?

The uniqueness of each of the known salt lakes is apparent not just to a biologist's practiced eye, but to anyone's. The biological singularity is just a part of a broader principle. The mood of each lake is entirely its own, as if each were inhabited by its separate demon.

Medusa Lake is a universe of jellyfish medusae. Little else lives there. The lake is deep, and the medusae hang at every level, as far down as the eye can see. They are arranged patternlessly, like snowflakes arrested in midfall. Their bells pulse strongly, but do not seem to move the medusae much. They just hold position. Their whitish color catches all the light available underwater and radiates it. The nearer medusae are in sharp focus, the far ones blurred, but all burn bright against the green universe of the lake. Swimming in the lake, a visitor feels the jellyfish slip against his skin and past. Their touch is cool and convinces the visitor, finally, that he is not drifting with some galaxy. The name Medusa Lake is Owen's, and is not on any map.

Snapper Lake is dominated by red and spotted snappers. The lake is long and narrow. Contouring its shore is a flat, swampy margin where land-building mangroves, in arching out their lattices of aerial prop roots, and in dropping their leaves, and in falling themselves in time, are reclaiming the lake. The Snapper Lake mangroves are an uncommon species called by Palauans *kodenges* and by Americans oriental mangrove. The slender trunks rise very straight and tall before branching. Because the canopy is high, it is possible for a man on the ground to see deep into the forest. Lakes shored by the shorter and more common *denges* do not allow such vistas. For anyone familiar with the squatter and more common mangrove forest, it is hard to believe at first that so vertical a world could be made by mangroves. The leaves are mangrove leaves, all right, but they look strange way up there. The forest of trunks might belong to lodgepole pines were it not for an occasional tropical epiphyte growing midway up (and indeed, Palauans used kodenges trees just as American Indians used lodgepoles).

The Snapper Lake forest is accessible by foot, for fallen trees make bridges over the mud and over the armies of spiked pneumatophores that rise from it, allowing the trees to breathe. A man can walk entirely around the lake on fallen logs. In the course of his walk he passes natural nurseries of mangrove seedlings, with the plants in each of a uniform age and height. Some nurseries are just beginning; some are well along. From time to time the green dart of a mangrove pod detaches itself in the treetops and whistles lethally down to half-bury itself in the mud.

Tropic birds argue high over the lake, burning motes in the sun, or they drop down near the shady surface and extinguish themselves in the shadows. Micronesian pigeons call from the forest. Their deep croaking roar is not like a bird's at all, or like the call of any other creature in existence. They sound like carnivorous forest toads stalking you and getting closer. Out on the lake in twos and threes, the lazy fins of mullet ruffle the water.

As the tide drops in the lagoon outside, a current in the lake begins to run westward, draining through passageways to the lagoon. All the lake's floating leaves drift toward its western end. The leaves gather there and mill slowly about. The current flows past the leaves and other debris, which are held back by a natural strainer of mangrove roots, and the water of the outlet is clear. Just before it vanishes, the current flows pellucidly and shallowly over a bottom of brown and golden mangrove leaves. In latitudes visited by autumn, this bottom would be called autumnal. Small snappers flit over the autumnal bottom. Apparently they grow here until large enough to venture safely into deeper water. Here and there in the outlet lie fallen mangrove logs, speckled by what looks from a distance like mildew. Up close, the mildew becomes clusters of small anemones. Their sessile parts have the palest blush of pink, as if some parasite has bled them nearly white. Their insubstantial tentacles stir in the stream.

The outlet is the best place for a snorkeler to enter the lake, for everywhere else the mangrove prop roots fence him out. The snorkeler steps bravely into shallow water, onto what appears a firm bottom of leaves. His foot expects the hardness of an autumn forest floor, or at very least the grudging resistance of mud, but his foot meets nothing at all and plunges, as if through a deadfall or an illusion. The bottom is not a bottom, but a loose and watery suspension in which the golden leaves have found their level. The snorkeler sinks until he finds his own level at thigh or hip. He begins to walk.

From the epicenter of each of his footfalls, shock waves run out in all directions along the bottom. The ground swells displace and lift the mangrove leaves, and from beneath them boil red clouds of a large-grained, foul-smelling sediment. When the water is deep enough for him to swim, the snorkeler gladly does so.

At its eastern end, uptide, Snapper Lake has two surfaces. Beneath the first, a thin upper lens of clear water, lies a second surface, a plane of cloudy white sediment. The interval between surfaces is seldom more than a foot. The plane of sediment is eerie. It flows like heavy gas over a table, wispy in places, like the dry-ice moor fogs of old scary movies. The sediment surface is immaterial. The snorkeler can pass his hand through it without immediately disturbing the sediment. Then, after a long delay, the sediment responds to the current his hand has created. Floating prone, the snorkeler feels himself pressed between the two planes. In places the clear lens narrows to an inch or two, and here he feels flattened out of existence. Close above him is a silvery surface, close below a ghostly one. Ahead the water of the lens seems unnaturally clear, but behind, roiled by the passage of his body, the two layers have mixed and the water is blurred and marbled. This is reassuring to the snorkeler, proof that he has some substance.

A juvenile snapper materializes from time to time. It pauses with pectoral fins spread. The snorkeler, too, pauses in midstroke. Man and fish stare at one another for a moment. Then the fish snaps its tail and vanishes into the silty plane, like a ghost passing through a door.

At first there is an uneasiness in not knowing what lives below the surface of the sediment. There are no crocodiles in the lake, the Palauans say, but how can they be certain? Suppose this lake's crocodile was too small, before today, to eat a human, and therefore kept itself hidden? But when the snorkeler has swum the length of the lake and returned without being seized from below, he relaxes. There are no large crocodiles or anything else hungry or dangerous in the lake, he has proved by offering himself; but what animals do live in the sediment cloud? What is life like down there?

IN THE SOUTHERN ELABAOB ISLANDS, at the bottom of an irregular bowl of jungle-covered limestone, there is a third lake; circular, deep, and nameless. The lake's shoreline is undercut all the way around, a continuous overhanging cliff. A visitor must lower his air tanks and cameras by rope, and then dive from the cliff, or climb down one of several clefts, using roots and saplings as handholds. No single species dominates this lake. There is such a variety that John Kochi has called this Mixed-Up Lake. The lake's larger fish coast along the shore in a circling, one-way procession; surgeonfish and goatfish, traveling in schools, and occasionally a solitary barracuda. The barracuda, as it passes the snorkeler, swivels an eye back to study him. When the snorkeler slaps the water, the barracuda and the rest of the startled parade dart forward thirty feet or so, then slow to their former pace. The lake's smaller fish stick to the shore. The overhanging cliff is riddled with underwater caves and crevices which the small fish use as protection. Big-eyed squirrelfish stare out from the cave entrances. Cardinalfish haunt the honeycombed limestone of the walls. Sardine-sized halfbeaks with bills like needles, red sometimes, as if the owner had just run somebody through, follow the shoreline in large schools.

Beneath the lake's encircling cliff, supporting its underwater walls just as desert dunes buttress mesas, is a slope of silt. Sage-colored seaweed grows in scattered clumps along the slope, and as the snorkeler passes, frightened fish dart like jackrabbits from clump to clump. The snorkeler seldom sees the fish, just clouds of silt that mark their paths. The clouds hang like the dust a land animal might raise, but in the water it lingers longer.

As the snorkeler propels himself with hands and feet along the slope, his palms and soles pick up spicules from siliceous sponges, and he notices small pains, as if from tiny shards of glass; pains so threadlike they hardly seem pains at all.

There is a fourth salt lake in which all emissaries from land suffer a sea change. All along the shore, mangrove prop roots, slender above water, blossom at waterline with a submarine Spanish moss and grow downward in massive mossy colonnades. Living branches that dip underwater are encrusted with mussels, and dead branches that have fallen into deeper waters are covered with dark-green algae that bejewel themselves with an antidew of oxygen bubbles. Anything that dips or falls into the lake is transformed as if by magic.

A fifth salt lake seems at first glance a desert. Underwater, there is little in the middle distance to see. The lake's center holds only a few small mullet and a jack or two. The barrenness in that direction forces a visitor to look the other way, at the limestone and sparse corals of the shore, and it is here that the lake lives in miniature—in transparent shrimp that wave long, nearly invisible arms ahead of them, and small gobies that hug the rock so tightly they seem to be walking over it.

A sixth lake is a kingdom of date mussels. Every inch of the lake's containing walls is countersunk with round mussel holes. The lake's floor, a shallow thirty feet deep, is a pavement of old mussel shells. As a snorkeler swims along the shore wall, the bivalves ahead, sensing his approach, close up by the hundreds. The flicker of their closing motion precedes him like a shadow.

IF, IN ANY of Palau's salt lakes, you swim out several yards from shore, force most of the air from your lungs, and allow yourself to sink, stopping at a depth of two or three feet, just before that point at which the surface turns silver, and then look upward through your face mask, the entire lake is mirrored above. The water surface acts as a fish-eye lens. The lake's rim of hills wavers above, a green circumference, and it encloses a blue disk of sky. Bright puffs of cloud shimmer there, and sometimes a sunstruck white bird, a tropic bird or a tern—the lake's surface is never still enough to tell which. It is to this magic circle that Robert Owen would like to retire.

On some future morning, Owen, cigarette dangling from lips, will enter the biology lab office. If things work as he plans, the Chief Conservationist of the Trust Territory will be John Kochi, who will look up from Owen's old desk. Demei Otobed, the chief entomologist, will look up from his own desk. One of them will say, "Good morning, Rubak. What can we do for you?" Owen will request permission to set up his camp on one of the salt lakes. The lakes will be protected by then, Owen hopes, and permission will be necessary. Kochi will grant it readily. Today both Kochi and Otobed feel some resentment about their years as natives under Owen, the colonial officer, but not so much resentment that they will take revenge when roles are reversed.

⟿ 18

JOHN KOCHI, patrolling for poachers, turns south into the maze of the elabaob islands. He aims at the midpoint of a long, hummocky peninsula, steering a collision course, but as the boat races near, the peninsula opens up. What seemed a single shoreline resolves itself first into headlands, then into islands, as from behind the headlands narrow channels speed into view, insinuating and separating what seemed solid. When he has passed through the first peninsula, Kochi changes course for another, and it, too, scatters before him. The effect has inspired a Palauan proverb. *Ngkora Ngeruduid el keketut engdi kakengesakl,* "it is like the Seventy Islands, which seem to be single but are really many." It is hard to know how Kochi finds his way.

The islands are all much alike. They are big or little, near or far, but otherwise the same. The elabaob shapes are beautiful and are different, but not beautiful and different in a way that makes them distinguishable. The islands all rise in the same steep, swelling curve. The archetype recurs everywhere. Traveling among its doubtful permutations is like wandering in a house of mirrors. As the boat winds its way through, the traveler's eye seeks out the small things that diverge from the pattern; a windrow of yellow leaves on the water or a distant pair of tropic birds, white specks against the elabaob green, spiraling upward like leaves on the wind. The longer one's acquaintance with them, the less one really sees the islands. Perhaps this is how Palauan boatmen find their way, their problem solved as soon as the geometry of the course headings becomes the real thing and the islands just abstractions, pleasant dreams that slide away to either side.

With his throttle twisted as far as it will go, Kochi unravels the labyrinth. The channels between islands are shallow, and coral heads are scattered over the near, sandy bottom. The coral heads speed at the boat and disappear rapidly behind. The boat passes in a flash from sun to shadow, running close to an undercut limestone wall. For an instant there is the cool spelean smell of limestone, of wet rock, and then the boat flashes into the sunshine again.

Kochi passes an elabaob cove and, seeing something in it, abruptly slows. He turns and heads back through the cove's narrow entrance. An empty boat is tied to the steep inner shore. Kochi steers for it. "Poachers," he murmurs. The water under his boat goes turquoise, then grades smoothly into the yellow-white of the sandy bottom. Kochi cuts his motor and poles the boat in, seizing the poacher's gunwale as he comes alongside. He wears his samurai frown. This samurai frown for poachers is not much different from his frown against the sun, but something in the quality of his silence, as he examines the gear in the boat, suggests that he is very angry. He is also puzzled. He does not recognize the boat. He catches up a speargun from the seat. It is like any number of spearguns in Palau, and it gives no clue to the identity of its owner. He opens a battered Styrofoam ice chest and peers in. Nothing there. Finally, under the boat's tiny forward deck, he finds an old shirt. He turns the shirt over in his hands and nods. "I know who it is," he says. "It's a policeman here, a constable."

The constable is somewhere in the forest shooting pigeons and is likely to be there for some time. Fortunately Kochi knows which pier the man uses and decides to wait for him there.

The conservation officer jumps back into his boat. He yanks his starter cord and pulls away. When he is clear of the cove the samurai frown departs. Small, choppy waves sprint toward the boat, pass beneath, and recede as rapidly behind. Ahead, in shifting, fine-textured patches, the waves are flattened by gusts of wind. The water is darkened by the gusts, as if by cloud shadows or by God's spirit moving upon the face of the waters. Kochi can see the gusts before he feels them. He would have time to hold his hat down, if he wore a hat. The wind markings and Kochi race together. The instant he enters the flattened zone, a wall of wind strikes his face.

AT HIS DESK in the biology lab office John Kochi sometimes gets sleepy. He is never sleepy, he has noticed, in his boat. Patrolling alone on the water, Kochi is preoccupied by a single thought. He does not daydream. If he remembers that Ramona has no food at home, he puts out a trolling line, but the line requires little attention and does not divert him. Kochi never reminisces.

"My first thinking is to catch poachers," he says.

Kochi does not just drive around. This, in his opinion, is the mistake made by the marine conservationist and the three marine wardens who work for fisheries. Kochi is terrestrial conservation officer, and the water is not properly his domain, but the marine conservationist has never arrested anyone, so Kochi considers the ocean his by default. Since expanding his operations, and without any wardens of his own, Kochi has made many arrests on the water, to the indignation of both the arrestees and the marine conservationist. Kochi never just puts in time on the lagoon. He is always thinking of ways to catch poachers. Once his method was to spread false rumors about his patrol route that day, then go in the opposite direction. Once he painted the sides of his boat different colors. "That can't be Kochi," a fish poisoner would think, as a yellow speedboat bore down on him. The poisoner would hesitate, Clorox bottle in hand, waist deep in his illegal, lazy, and destructive method of fishing. "It can't be Kochi, because Kochi just went by here in a black boat." This trick did not work for long, of course, but as soon as the poachers got wise Kochi abandoned it for another. His favorite method for catching pyromaniacs is to buy candy for children and exchange it for information.

Kochi must be devious, for he is the only enforcement officer for Palau's 188 square miles of jungle and savannah, and the only man inclined to make arrests on all her leagues of lagoon and reef. His adversaries are men like himself, with Spartan boyhoods and roots in the subsistence life. Kochi must be ingenious, for they are.

Palauan fish bombers have discovered, through experiment, that old buckets can be used to muffle their explosions. By placing the bucket upside down on floats and attaching the dynamite to a long line beneath, they deaden the sound and increase their kill. The bombers go out on bamboo rafts and return in superficial innocence, but beneath their bamboo decks, on long lines strung through hundreds of gills, is their contraband catch. A visitor to the biology lab once asked if rigid control of dynamite sales might stop the fish bombing. Kochi replied that rigid locks would be necessary too, for otherwise Palauans would just steal their explosives. At the time he was working with the Koror constabulary on a case of dynamite theft. "The stolen dynamites mystery is still at large, and person(s) suspected unknown," he had written in his most recent report. If dynamite were not available, Kochi added, the fish bombers would turn to the World War II ordnance that is still abundant in Palau. Fish bombers are skillful, though not quite infallible, at defusing bombs and shells and extracting the explosives without setting them off.

"And you would have to stop selling these," Kochi concluded, holding up a box of Tsubame brand wooden matches. He explained that Palauan fish bombers shave the heads off hundreds of matches, pack them tightly in pomade jars, and rig homemade fuses that burn underwater. Kochi set the matchbox down again. He did not try to conceal his admiration for his countrymen.

Bombing, like Clorox poisoning, is an unselective method, a broadside attack on the whole ecosystem. It damages the coral and thus kills the goose for its golden egg, for without coral, reef fish cease to be a replenishable resource. But bombing does at least require imagination.

There are ways to discourage the practice, Kochi believes, better ways than just stumbling on the bomber in the act. Kochi has done this, but it depends too much on luck. In dynamited fish the ribs are dislocated slightly. With small fish like sardines, a quick autopsy is difficult, but with larger fish it is easy. The manager of the Palau Fishermen's Cooperative will not accept dynamited fish. The bombers sell to small stores instead, and Kochi plans to visit these regularly when he finds the time.

The conservation laws of the Trust Territory are Kochi's Old Testament. He enforces them to the letter. He believes that if he ever made an exception, everyone would hear about it. Palau is a small place, and word travels fast. "I won't give anyone a chance, not even my own brother," he says happily. Such a policy is unusual in Palau, where officials tend to overlook the misdemeanors of members of their family or clan. It is not easy for Kochi—his former best friend is now an enemy after an arrest—but Kochi sees no other way. "When I catch someone destroying my place, I have to apprehend him," he says.

Once Kochi was passing behind a house when, from within, he heard the owner address his wife. "Get me my gun, I'm going hunting." Walls are very thin in Palau, and Kochi heard this distinctly. He waited outside and confronted the man as he emerged. "Where are you going?" Kochi asked. "To hunt birds," the man replied boldly, aware of his rights. "What kind of birds?" Kochi asked, for pigeons were out of season at the time. There are few other edible birds in Palau, and the man could not think of an innocent name. "Just my chicken," he answered lamely. "Go ahead and shoot him then," said Kochi. The man was rattled. He would later sadly tell a friend that he was giving up poaching. He had only to *think* of pigeons, he said, and Kochi knew about it. The man saw no recourse now but to shoot his chicken. Kochi's handling of the matter would have pleased the old Hebrews.

Once Kochi brought charges against the marine conservationist for taking undersized turtles. This was a sensational accusation, and it caused a considerable commotion before Robert Owen, in the interest of peace between his conservation department and that of fisheries, smoothed it over. The marine conservationist, on learning of the charges, protested that the turtles had been captured for use in an experiment. Kochi replied that the law provided no exceptions for experimental use. Just because a man was marine conservationist, Kochi said, did not entitle him to violate conservation laws.

The marine conservationist, normally an unctuous and calculating man, lost his temper.

"But you're eating pigeons!" he shouted.

"Who told you that?" asked Kochi.

"The pigeon hunters you arrest! They know you eat the pigeons you confiscate!"

"How can that be? They are preserved in formalin."

Kochi led the marine conservationist to the lab insectary, where all his evidence, tagged and labeled, was arrayed on a table. There were three pairs of zoris left behind by poachers who fled barefoot into the jungle; one undersized green turtle confiscated from an American woman; several large jars filled with formalin and dynamited fish, their dead eyes staring outward; a number of uneaten pigeons; and one straw hat with red hatband, tagged: "Evidense for suspected pigeon poacher(s) / March 9, 1971 / A Japanese hat." This evidentiary hat was exactly like the hat Kochi sometimes wears, only newer and crisper. The poacher must have dropped it shortly after buying it. A lesser man than Kochi, or a more humorous one, might have considered a switch.

The marine conservationist was speechless, baffled by the table's display of rectitude. He had never doubted that Kochi ate confiscated pigeons; what could be more natural? It is easy to sympathize with the marine conservationist and be baffled along with him. Where did all Kochi's rectitude come from? In Kochi's life the church has not loomed large. As a boy he was, on his own mother's testimony, a liar. None of Kochi's friends or colleagues has the answer. Kochi himself can't explain it.

Gossip is epidemic on small islands, worse even than in small towns, but there is very little gossip about Kochi in Palau. His dedication to conservation consumes him so that he has had no time, or room, to develop a kinky side. He is a disappointment to the gossips, they speak resentfully of his sinlessness.

SOMETIMES KOCHI WORRIES that he is trading too much on his old reputation. His adversaries are, after all, men with guns who watch from the jungle as he confiscates their hats and zoris. It is only their memories of the young Singer, the present Singer believes, that keeps them from pulling their triggers. Kochi does not feel so tough as all that, anymore. Lately he has found to his dismay that he is afraid to really put his arm into spanking his children. Fights no longer interest him much. "Now I think I'm a good man," he says. "I don't get so mad." A part of his nature seems to have died. Kochi's change from hoodlum-warrior to public servant, to gentle father and friend, is the one truly puzzling fact of a straightforward life, and Kochi himself is puzzled. There must be some of the fervor of the convert in his present mildness, but not enough to explain it entirely. Kochi assumes that someday he will be tested by the men he pursues, and he hopes he will pass.

It is likely that he will. The pigeon poachers, hidden in the jungle and peering down their barrels at him, are probably more correct in their judgment of Kochi than Kochi is himself. The conservation officer is in no position, naturally, to see the Samurai frown on his own brow. Spirit may have softened in Kochi, but reflexes are still the same. Recently, in the first flush of anger at hearing that a Palauan judge had let off three fish dynamiters with small fines, Kochi announced that he was going to hunt the men down one at a time, beat them, and then turn himself in. "Don't do that, John," Robert Owen advised, and Kochi decided that Owen was right.

Shortly after this incident, in concluding a report on a group of poachers who had eluded him, Kochi wrote a sentence that would have given the poachers pause, if they had heard rumors of his savage boyhood.

"I do not know their names," he wrote, "but when I see them I know their faces."

Part
Four

⟶ 19

IN THE MAIL one morning Owen received word that his Trust Territory contract had been renewed again. He would be employed in Palau for another two years. The news worked on him the way the horse capsule of hydrocarbon had once worked on his hookworm. A great weight was lifted. There were people at headquarters on Saipan who had wanted to see Owen's service ended, and for the past weeks Owen had been in suspense, suspecting that a move was afoot to oust him. Demei Otobed had noticed Owen's nervousness. "He can't pin small insects," Demei had observed. "He destroys them."

"My anxiety level has been high," Owen confessed, now that the wait was over.

Owen was suddenly full of plans. He would do all the things he had wanted to, but had been afraid to begin. He would consolidate the conservation programs of all six districts of the Trust Territory. He would lobby to gain more control for his office over big public-works projects, especially those that included reef blasting, dredging, and other large-scale alterations of the environment. He would export his Palauan council-of-chiefs conservation program to the rest of the Trust Territory.

Owen decided to celebrate by taking his wife and some Americans in the government to a salt lake. The lake had interested him for some time.

He had seen it from the air but had never visited. Until now he had not felt like making the trip.

As a dry run Owen took the conservation patrol boat out to the outer reef. It was his first voyage in many months, and he was rusty. On returning to the pier he tied the boat up wrong, and it sank with the next high tide. John Kochi, grumbling, refloated it. "I'm ashamed to show my face in the office," Owen said the next day as he drove his small party of Americans to the dock. "I used to run all around these islands in a small boat."

This morning Owen had trouble finding the release button that lets you tip the outboards down into the water. One of his passengers found it for him. Then Owen had difficulty getting the motors into neutral and reverse. Palauan fishermen in other boats watched, and some smiled. Owen suffered in silence, making just one complaint about the stiffness of the controls. They were stiff indeed. Once clear of the dock, he did better. He had not forgotten where the channel ran through Iwayama Bay.

The climb up from the bay, over the limestone-and-jungle divide, and down to the salt lake was short, but the descent was steep. Hera Owen, who is very light on her feet, made it easily. The other American wife, with some coaxing and guidance, followed with legs trembling. Everyone sat on the shore and stripped down to their swimming things. Owen entered the water first. The lake was forty minutes from his bungalow door, but so far as he knew, no man had been here before.

The new lake had nearly as many jellyfish as Medusa Lake, but here the jellyfish were not so striking. They were mud-colored, like the bottom, and they had spherical attachments on their tentacles, which, after the simplicity of the jellyfish in Medusa Lake, seemed tasteless ornament, like fins on Cadillacs.

Owen swam without a snorkel, and one of his guests asked why.

"They annoy me," Owen answered. "Besides, I'm under the influence of a man called Bronson, who didn't believe in them. He didn't even use a mask in fact. He dove with homemade goggles. His theory was they trapped less air, so you could dive deeper with them."

Owen's arms are too spindly for his torso, a common occurrence in once-wiry men who have put on weight at their middles. He swam with what seemed an awkward stroke, but it moved him fast enough. The jellyfish became thicker and thicker around Owen as he neared the center of the lake. He batted them aside with his long ungainly strokes. From a soup of jellyfish he looked back at his companions. "They're thicker'n hell out here!" he shouted.

If the theme of Snapper Lake, with its ghostly plane of sediment, is surreal, and the theme of Medusa Lake cosmic, then this new lake's theme was decadence. The muck of the bottom was cobwebbed with a fungusy white lace. Fallen mangrove branches were covered funereally with purple-brown sponge. The medusae floated like dusty brown chandeliers in a haunted mansion. There seemed to be little competition among species and little vigor. The ocean had deserted the lake, leaving it sparsely populated with thanatoid forms.

"Depauperate," said Owen.

Whatever else the lake meant to him, he kept it to himself. He commented briefly on how many of the lake's life forms depended on mangrove prop roots and fallen logs. He pointed silently several times to the broken mussel shells that lay here and there on the bottom. They seemed to interest him especially, for some reason. When someone swam up with something for identification, Owen would give the name a little gruffly. He did not show off his knowledge. If he did not know a name, he said so without John Kochi's sad pause.

One American dove twenty feet to the bottom and came up with one of the green plants that grew there. Owen looked it over, and said that he had never seen it before. It was an alga of some kind, he thought. Then a second American, who was exploring near shore, shouted that he had seen a fish.

"What was it? A snapper?" called Owen.

"No, it's a coelacanth-looking fish."

Owen was impatient with that description, but amused by it. He did not see anything himself, for out in the middle of the lake, where Owen now swam, there was nothing to see of fleeing fish but the explosions of sediment they made each time they brushed bottom. Each explosion sent up a nacreous shrapnel of mussel-shell fragments. The fragments shivered downward and settled out, leaving the puffs of sediment to hang awhile, like smoke after the fireworks. But then Owen came to the shallow water near shore, and he confronted a coelacanth-looking fish for the first time. The fish lay on an algae-covered log, thinking it was hidden, though just its mid-parts were covered by algae. Head and tail were exposed. Only when Owen moved to pinch the coelacanth by the tailfin did the fish realize its naked-ness and shoot off. Owen smiled after it.

"You called it a coelacanth, and I'm about ready to go along," he said to the American. "I've never seen anything like it."

"It might be a new species, then?"

"Yes, it might very well be."

Toward the end of the afternoon, Owen, waist-deep in water, called from a forest of mangrove prop roots. "I've got a silverfish of some kind over here," he said, but before his companions reached him he changed that. "No, they're crustaceans. Amphipods."

When the others arrived they saw nothing.

"Watch when I put my hand around," Owen said. He reached behind the prop roots and, just as he had anticipated, the amphipods scuttled around from the far side. They had been hiding there. Amphipods, like squirrels, prefer to keep wood between themselves and possible enemies. The amphipods looked like squat, wet silverfish with big eyes. Owen's companions clustered around him, looking at his amphipods and wondering, perhaps, why he found them so interesting. Owen himself was already looking away, scanning the far shoreline for the next thing.

"This place is full of life," he said, more to the lake itself than to his friends.

THE NEXT MORNING Owen was in his office at seven, before his staff ar-rived. He had not showed up so early for a long time. He was flipping through *The Marine Life and Fresh Water Fishes of Ceylon*, looking for the coelacanth. He could not find it, but he satisfied himself that the fish was a goby of some kind. "That's the family, anyway," he said. None of the draw-ings of Ceylonese gobies was quite right. None had the coelacanth mouth or the feathery caudal fin that yesterday had followed each coelacanth like a shroud. Perhaps it really was a new species.

"My legs are a little stiff," Owen said, "but I sure slept well last night." His face was relaxed and seemed less deeply lined. He wanted to talk.

"Coelacanth Lake and Medusa Lake are less than a mile apart, as the crow flies," he said (the new lake now had a name), "yet look at how different they are. Why are mussels predominant in Coelacanth and tunicates in Medusa? How did those mussel shells get broken and spread out over the bottom? Were the gobies eating them? I could understand if the log bearing the mussels collapsed and they smothered there, but why were they all broken?"

Owen ruminated for a while.

"I think I'll stop calling them salt lakes. They should be called *marine* lakes. 'Salt lakes' is misleading. There are real salt lakes in the world—Great Salt Lake, the Caspian Sea—lakes that have salt deposits."

Owen ruminated again.

"Plankton might be the best indicator of the diversity some of these smaller forms are very fast evolving. I'll bet there's never been a plankton net in any of those salt lakes. But no, come to think of it, I suppose the larger fish will be better indicators. The larger forms are more effectively trapped. It's harder for them to get to the sea."

THAT EVENING, Owen, still celebrating the renewal of his contract, and perhaps also his exploration of the lake, took his wife to the hotel for drinks. He was brashly confident. He had forgotten, it seemed, that his contract renewal was a reprieve and not a pardon. He had a job in Palau for another two years, and then another day of reckoning, but he did not think of that. He looked out from the veranda at the sinuous coves of Iwayama Bay. A fisherman in a bamboo raft was poling homeward, leaving a narrow wake on the smooth surface, colored now by evening. The bay's elabaob promontories and islands were soft green in the evening light. No newcomer could have guessed how sharp the limestone was underneath.

Hera Owen asked her husband whether he would concentrate, now that he was sure of his job, on any one bird or animal.

"No!" he answered, in triumph and contentment. "I'll be just like Charles Darwin. A worm in one hand, and a . . ."

Owen paused to think what Darwin held in his other hand, but could not. He improvised. ". . . And a dinosaur egg in the other."

20

SHORT, neat stacks of papers ran the entire length of the workbench in the biology lab office. There were GI benefit documents, X-ray plates, health inventory forms, confirmation of financial resources forms, admission forms. John Kochi had applied for admission to four colleges, and the stacks were the necessary paperwork. "I don't know how the kids do it," said Robert Owen, who was handling most of the details for Kochi. "It's driving me half crazy. God, it'll be a relief when we get rid of John."

Demei Otobed agreed. "I've never written so many letters in my life," he said.

Kochi's life history was laid out on the workbench. The documents, in the curious way of documents, seemed to make the man more real. There was a transcript of grades from George Washington High School, Agaña, Guam. The transcript was partial. "Subsequent to my graduation," explained Kochi in a covering note, "a severe typhoon destroyed the school and some records, including my record of grades and graduation from the school. The enclosed affidavit is the best I can do concerning my high-school records." On the transcript Kochi's old names were out of order, "John Ngiraingas Singer," and his date of birth was three years early. In Micronesia the facts in certain categories tend to wander. In ninth and tenth grades, according to the transcript, Kochi got As in agriculture, art, and physical education, and Ds in algebra and civics.

There was an honorable discharge for Sp. 4 John S. Ngiraingas, ER 50 009 211, with a note from Colonel Eugene S. Tarr, AGC, Commanding. "I trust that you will always retain pleasant memories of your active Army and Reserve service," the Colonel wrote, "and that you will continue to render loyal service to the National Defense through your community and business relations."

There was Civil Action No. 1070, District Court for the Palau District:

> In the matter of Changing the Last Name of John Singer Ngiraingas:
>
> This matter having come on for a hearing upon the petition of John Singeru Ngiraingas, filed herein on June 10, 1964, praying to this court to enter a decree changing his last name to be KOCHI.
>
> The petitioner, John Singeru Ngiraingas, was born on August 28, 1937, in Ngchesar Municipality, Palau District, Western Caroline Islands, Trust Territory of the Pacific Islands, out of wedlock of Kochi (now deceased) and Obeketakl.
>
> Ngiraingas is the petitioner's step-father.
>
> It is ORDERED, ADJUDGED, and DECREED that John Singeru Ngiraingas' name be changed to read as JOHN SINGERU KOCHI.

There were copies of John's marriage certificate and the birth certificates of his four children. On the marriage certificate, his mother's signature looked like the work of a right-handed child practicing with her left. Obeketakl had trouble keeping her name on the line, and the last letters plunged under it. Her son's signature on all the documents was brave and violent and full of flourish.

Kochi now knew for certain that he was to leave. The message of the workbench and its stacks of papers was inescapable. There had been doubt, earlier, that the money necessary for his education would be raised, but now, through the efforts of Owen and several stateside Americans who had met Kochi in Palau and had been impressed by him, there were guarantees of more than enough. Kochi would be going to one of several small colleges in California, the only question was which. Kochi seemed preoccupied by the knowledge. He wore his samurai frown on days when there was no sun to stare into.

"I'm worried about what will happen to Stevie," Kochi said. "He never obeys his mother, only me." Kochi considered making a will and leaving everything to his son. Under the Palauan system his daughters would be taken care of, he said. "He's the only son I've got, so don't spoil him," Kochi told his wife—a strange request, for it was never she who spoiled him. Kochi worried too about Ramona and how she would support the family. Under Palau's complex system of clan and family obligations, requests for aid must be made boldly, and he worried that Ramona would not be able to do so.

And Kochi worried about failing in college. His colleagues at the biology lab were worried about that themselves. Demei Otobed predicted, without sounding convinced, that the next four years would be hard for Kochi, but that he would make it, if he applied himself. Demei might have been troubled by memories of the unofficial story hour at the biology lab, during which he read to Kochi from scientific journals. He had often had to stop and translate an English phrase to Palauan. "First and foremost in the economic sphere . . ." he would quote, from a Jacques Cousteau statement on pollution of the world's oceans. "Wait a minute," Kochi would say. "Go back. I don't understand that."

Owen made no predictions. The biggest problem, he thought, would be Kochi's written English. Kochi had made progress lately, but he suffered relapses. "It was the most coherent awarding catastrophy to our staff of Entomology-Conservation Departments," he had written recently in a note to Palau's high-school principal. "Our admiration to you may be demolished but the fact and results of your help will remain our guidance. Your servant always, John S. Kochi, Conservationist." Owen wondered what a California English instructor would make of that.

Kochi was unprepared in other ways. He had strange notions about what his life in California would be like. He had served American academic men for so long as porter and workhorse diver that he assumed it would continue to be so. "If they want me to dive, they have to furnish me a wet suit," he said, for he had heard about the cold waters of the North Pacific. "I'll tell them we don't need to use wet suits in Palau."

Kochi planned to play baseball for his college team. He was certain he would lose weight once he was away from Palauan cooking and that he would soon be in playing trim. If any of the young Californians doubted his abilities as a ballplayer, John, the most dangerous left-handed power hitter in the Trust Territory, planned to show them his triple-A credit card. The card reads: "AAA-1 Credit Card, Holtzman's Jewelers, 19 Twelfth Street, Columbus, Georgia. This certifies that Sgt. John Graingas has been awarded AAA-1 Rating, with fullest credit privileges." On the back of the card, noted in pencil, is the number 48. That's all the card says. It does not mention that Kochi left Fort Benning on weekends to play ball for Holtzman's Jewelers, wearing uniform 48, an even number for good luck, as always in his baseball career. The baseball crowd in Columbus, Georgia, and across the bridge in Phoenix City, Alabama, called him Coconut. "Hey Coconut!" they shouted, as he rounded the bases after each home run. But the card says nothing about that, and its presentation to the baseball coach in California would surely cause puzzlement.

As his time grew short, Kochi began tieing up loose ends. He arranged with Douglas Faulkner that his brother, Jimmy Kochi, would take over as Faulkner's assistant and guide, and with this single stroke he took care of obligations to both men. He also suggested to Robert Owen that Jimmy be hired as conservation officer too. John was troubled that his departure might signal the commencement of a wildlife massacre, and he was anxious that his replacement be a tough man. Jimmy Kochi had the qualification, John thought. Jimmy is not just nuts, John believes, but "mean-nuts," the way John himself was as a young man. An eagle tattooed in blue—a memento of Jimmy's days as a sailor—spreads its wings across most of his broad chest. He usually needs a shave. He has only one good eye, having lost the other in a boyhood fishing accident. It happened when Jimmy and John, ages six and eight, were fishing for mullet with Japanese hand grenades. They had fished this way before and had learned that you must smash Japanese grenades before throwing them. This they did, but the grenades did not explode. John dove and retrieved one. He took it apart, laid the ingredients on a rock to dry in the sun, and warned Jimmy not to fool with them. He returned to the lagoon to spearfish. As soon as his older brother was in the water, Jimmy hit the fuse with a hammer. It exploded, wounding him in the face and chest. (In Micronesia this sort of delayed World War II injury is very common.) John carried Jimmy home and dumped him on the floor. "Jimmy blew himself up with a grenade," he told his mother. He remembers that he got a beating for not taking better care of his brother.

Now, twenty-five years later, John took the same brother down to the water near the old Japanese refrigeration building, to teach him scuba diving. It was a skill that Jimmy would need as Faulkner's assistant. John's instruction was simple. He helped Jimmy into a borrowed Aqua-lung, the two descended the ruined concrete steps of the Japanese dock, and they entered the water. John paused for a minute to teach his brother buddy breathing, and then they swam off to spearfish. They returned with several squirrelfish and a good-sized octopus, speared through the head. The brothers sat on the dock talking for a while, before John, as an afterthought, (there is no strong SPCA instinct in Palauan spearmen) killed the octopus. Avoiding the beak as he handled the octopus, John eviscerated it with the strength of his fingers. It proved to be no real act of grace, for the octopus departed life grudgingly. Thirty minutes passed before the strength of the suction cups began to fade, and another ten before the tentacles stopped pulsing with color.

On another day Kochi drove Number 35 Mitsubishi Diesel Jeep to the elementary school to register his son for the first grade. The four Palauan women who were handling the registration sat at a wooden table on the school's green playing field, above the blue ocean. As Kochi leaned over the table, making sure Stevie's name was spelled right, he frowned, as if into the sun or into a difficulty.

KOCHI CONTINUED to spend his weekends patrolling. It might have seemed proper that he spend his little remaining time with his family, but weekends are the best time to catch poachers, most of whom are employed in Koror during the week.

One Saturday of this period, Kochi patrolled northward along the eastern coast of Babeldaob, with a friend along for company. There was a storm to the north, and the headlands of Babeldaob's shoreline receded into mistiness. To the south the world was in full color, but northern Babeldaob was a study in grays. At the edge of the bad weather Kochi saw a small beach with human figures on it, and he headed there. The figures proved to be two middle-aged women. When Kochi was within hailing distance, he cut the motor.

"Where are your husbands?" he shouted in Palauan.

"We have no husbands," one of the women answered. "They have gone back to Koror. But you two come here, and we'll be one-and-one."

The invitation was not serious, apparently; Kochi grinned at the joke. At that moment several cockatoos, flawlessly white, flew up from the steep jungle behind the beach. They had been disturbed by something—poaching husbands, perhaps. Kochi saw no boat, however, and he decided to believe the women. Their husbands probably were back in Koror, as they said, and would be returning later for them.

Kochi yanked his starter cord and turned back into sunny weather. He drove past Koror and into the maze of the elabaob islands. He sped toward Urukthapel, the largest of the elabaob islands, steering a collision course; but at the last moment Urukthapel's single shoreline separated into many islands. Banking left, Kochi entered a long, narrow bay formed by a natural breakwater of small islands in front and Urukthapel proper behind. At the far end of the bay he abruptly cut his motor.

The sudden quiet made the memory of the motor very noisy. The noise had frightened seabirds from their perches in the forest canopy. Most of the birds now settled again into the trees, but a few continued to circle. Against the green of the surrounding jungle they were easier to see than against the sky. All were white, but the wings of different species beat at different rates, and the circles they inscribed had different radii. The bay was a favorite anchorage for poachers, and Kochi listened for gunshots. He heard none, just the calls of the seabirds. With the motor off, the birds had regained their voices. A great moon jellyfish, genus *Aurelia*, the largest but least substantial of Palau's jellyfish, drifted under the stern. The jellyfish was, like a daytime moon, nearly not there.

Kochi departed the bay and continued southward through the elabaob maze. He swerved into every cove, penetrating deeply enough to scan all of the cove's inner shoreline for anchored boats, then swerving out again. In the green water of one shallow cove, he passed over a spotted eagle ray, and he circled back for another look. The ray had been moving lazily, but with this second approach of the boat, it became alarmed, accelerated with amazing quickness, and with four beats of its wings was gone.

Now and again Kochi swung out from the islands, far out on the lagoon. He coasted the barrier reef, looking for fish dynamiters. He put out a trolling line, but had no luck at first. "They're not hitting," he said. "Maybe the water's too smooth." Then after a while he caught several rainbow runners. When he tired of his sorties into the lagoon he would reel in his handline and head back in.

Kochi saw his first boat on the small beach of a two-acre island. He pulled up alongside, and several Palauans standing on the beach welcomed him. They were acquaintances of Kochi's, all youngish men in business or government. They were having a picnic, not poaching. With them was a guest, a Chinese businessman from Guam, and for this man's benefit they spoke in English. One Palauan gestured at Kochi with a plucked chicken in either hand, then he split the birds and hung the halves underwater on the boat's anchor line, to get them salty.

"Where's the meat?" asked Kochi, as he stepped on the beach.

"What do you mean, 'Where's the meat?'" said a Palauan named Haruo. He stared at Kochi with mock anger, as if at a freeloader, and demanded, "Where's the fresh fish?"

"There'll be fresh fish," Kochi answered. He returned to his boat, and two of the Palauans grabbed their face masks and spearguns and jumped in after him. In half an hour the three men returned with three big boxfish—tough-skinned, with full pink lips—and one very large triggerfish, with the buck teeth of its species, and one large needlefish, and a number of smaller fish of various kinds.

"It's strange," Haruo said, watching as Kochi unloaded the catch. "This conservation officer of ours. He knows every corner. He knows exactly where to go to catch fish."

The Palauans cooked the triggerfish, the needlefish, and the split chickens on a makeshift grill of bamboo. They tossed the boxfish directly on the fire, where it blistered and blackened in the smoky, inefficient heat of sea-drifted, sun-dried coconut husks and bamboo, and of bark gathered from the casuarinas that stood above the beach. If this smoke is important to the recipe, it will be difficult to duplicate in another country. Several of the smaller fish were made into sashimi by one of the spearmen who had accompanied Kochi. He sliced the raw fish into a yellow plastic bowl, poured in soy sauce, halved a lime and squeezed seeds and all in afterward.

The food was nearly cooked when Kochi looked up and noticed that a boat had anchored at a neighboring island. He jogged to his patrol boat to investigate, and Haruo and another Palauan hurried after him. The conservation officer and his volunteer deputies left the beach at a gallop. The Chinese businessman, a slight, sad-eyed man with a tiny paunch, did not understand what was happening. He had not seen the other boat and did not know that Kochi was conservation officer. He nodded in the direction of the rapidly diminishing speedboat. "That's the life they love," he said good-naturedly. "They don't care about advancement." The businessman said he no longer made trips to the outer islands of the Trust Territory because the people out there were even worse and never bought anything.

The suspected boat proved innocent, and Kochi and his party returned just as lunch was declared ready. The men peeled back the blackened hide of the boxfish and ate the white flesh that clung to its inner surface. There was taro, a big pot of rice, a jar of Japanese pickled cabbage, two drinking coconuts, an ice chest full of Coke, root beer, strawberry pop, grape pop, and cherry pop. They ate everything with their hands. Kochi declared that box-fish was his favorite, but he seemed to spend as much time eating sashimi and chicken. It was funny how much sashimi you could eat, he said reflectively.

When the men finished, they talked.

Haruo, who lived on Guam now and was returning to Palau only for business, told his countrymen how badly his children spoke Palauan.

"Jesus. They sound just like . . . *Yapese*! Like Yapese trying to talk Palauan!"

Haruo and Kochi looked at each other, shook their heads, and laughed. Kochi told Haruo not to worry. In Ponape his own oldest children had spoken only Ponapean, Kochi said, and when they returned to Palau they couldn't run with the other kids, at first, but soon they relearned their native tongue. Today they didn't remember a single Ponapean word.

Kochi mentioned that he would soon be going to school in California.

Everyone was interested. Haruo said that he had been to that state. "It's all right, except for the rush hour," Haruo said, and he told everyone about the rush hour in California. Listening, Kochi did not look happy. He had seen American traffic in his army days, but he had never really become involved with it. The army had insulated him; he knew stateside barracks, but he did not really know the States.

"I hate crowds," Kochi said. "I just don't like it. But I think it will be all right if I get in a dormitory. I'll just stay in the dormitory until class, and after school I'll go straight back. The first thing I won't do, is drive."

"You have to," said Haruo. *"That's the only way you can get anyplace."*

The Palauans all laughed at the thought of such a system.

The conversation turned to Palau's original population and the effect of foreign diseases, and from that to the Hawaiian Islands and foreign diseases there. Three of the Palauans and the Chinese businessman had been to Hawaii, and now, pooling their knowledge of the place, they determined that the Hawaiian language was still spoken on the Big Island, on Maui, Lanai, and a little on Kauai. There were still some pure Hawaiians in each of those places. Then the men talked about pidgin. If you learned Hawaiian pidgin, said one man, you could understand the pidgin spoken in a certain part of New Guinea. (This was a very cosmopolitan group, for Palau, and Kochi seemed at home among them.) They spoke of the beauty of Hawaiian women. They spoke about haoles. Someone said that now 60 percent of Hawaii's population was haoles. Then they talked about cash economies and subsistence economies.

"I think this cash economy is the root of all evil," Kochi said. It was a funny line, a new version, but Kochi did not intend it that way. He spoke gravely, wearing the serious face he sometimes uses in giving the Latin names for plants.

The young Palauan businessmen were silent. The Chinese from Guam gazed ahead. Haruo sipped his Coke and stared, through half-lidded eyes, into the remains of the boxfish smoldering on the fire.

~~ 21

THE ENGLISH III class at Palau High School was asked recently to write a composition about a place—any place. The class was of eighth and ninth graders, intermediate students in English, and not the best at that language. Of all the places they had to write about, a third of the class picked the same one. The place they chose is tiny, but it is one of the centers of power in Palau.

"Kayangel is a small island that is far from Koror," wrote one student. "Kayangel is very beautiful. It has some beautiful beaches. They are very white and very much beautiful. . . ."

"Kayangel Island is so beautiful and pretty," wrote another, "because it's surrounded by the sea. The Kayangel Island is so small and it's a very good island. Because we just sit in our house and hear the sound of the weaves breaking the shore. . . ."

"Kayangel is a small Island far from Koror. It is a beautiful island in Palau. When I say beautiful It means It is a good & nice Place to live. It has so many birds, fish & some others. . . ."

The atoll of Kayangel is the northernmost inhabited land in Palau. Except for one small, bird-inhabited atoll to its northwest, it is the northernmost land of any kind. Kayangel's islands cannot quite be seen from the northern shore of Babeldaob, for the curve of the earth puts their highest palms just under the horizon. The trip by Yanmar boat from Koror to

Kayangel takes a full day. The largest island, and the only inhabited one, is called Kayangel, after which the whole atoll has its name. Kayangel Island is long and narrow, as atoll-islands tend to be, and it curves slightly, for its foundation is a segment of the reef's great circle. For someone standing on the inside of the island's curve, with his feet in the sand of the lagoon beach, the three smaller islands of the atoll lie close at hand on the arc to the south, progressively but only slightly diminished by distance. One student wrote of this arrangement, alluding to the atoll as he would to a ship, "Kayangel has her islands around her." At low tide it is possible to walk, on hard wave-patterned sand, from one island to another.

In almost every one of the English III essays on Kayangel there is a wistfulness about the place. In school young Palauans are taught that education and a cash economy mean the future. Koror, with its government salaries, Datsuns, Toyotas, bars, imitation nightclubs, and Saturday-night fights, is a glimpse of that future. No one in the class wanted to write about Koror. Kayangel, where the average annual income is fifty dollars—copra is the only cash crop—stands at the other pole of Palauan possibilities.

"We can't go back to the old ways," Palauan students often recite, but they don't seem entirely convinced. They do not have much help from the old people—even the oldest can't remember a time before the Japanese or Germans—and no Palauan Rousseau or Thoreau has articulated a school of thought to draw assurance from, so each student arrives at his doubts on his own.

"Palau in the present is very good because every man has the right to do something he wants and no body can stop him. But there are many troubles happening this time, but in the past it didn't. The people were very polite to the old men and the women but now they are not. . . ."

"Long time ago, Palau was different than this time. The people at that time didn't have education. Palau had beautiful big forests that had many different kinds of birds and animals. I think the people at that time wore something like the Yapese wear today. Today, Palau has almost improved for everything, because the people are educated so they can run their own government and make something to export and earn money for their government. But today we can't see many kinds of birds or animals, rather the land is destroyed."

Everyone's heart goes back to a time before his own memories, even as his intellect accepts the future the government has decided for him. Kayangel and her sister islands, Ngeriungs, Ngerbelas, and Orak, are islands in a geography of regret and hope.

"Kayangel is the smallest Municipality in Palau. It is located at the North of Palau. There are few people who live there. Kayangel is one of the most famous Municipality in Palau. Because the people of Kayangel are all participate with each other to do something good about their Municipality. In Kayangel there are two atoll islands located west of Kayangel. These two islands are called Orak and Ngerbelas. These two islands are the place where all birds in Palau lay their eggs. And there is a tree in Kayangel called Hibiscuss that is the biggest Hibiscuss tree in Palau. But if you break one of its stems the storm will come. There is a man in Kayangel, named Bardarii, that man can use a small paddle to make the storm, so that it won't come. . . ."

EIGHT MILES NORTHWEST of Kayangel there is a smaller atoll, Ngeruangel, the northernmost land of any kind in Palau. Ngeruangel too is a symbolic atoll. On the map it stands above Kayangel like an asterisk.

Ngeruangel's single island is a treeless spit of sand and coral boulders, inhabited only by nesting birds, but it was once, Palauans say, the home of a proud and cruel people who subjected Kayangel and parts of northern Babeldaob. The farmers of Kayangel paid tribute in crops to Ngeruangel, and the fishermen of Kayangel reserved for Ngeruangel their first-caught fish.

One day, the story goes, the small son of a Kayangelese fisherman named Redechor became hungry in his father's canoe and ate half of the first-caught fish. When a Ngeruangelese canoe pulled alongside, its captain saw that the law had been violated and he took the boy off. He placed the boy's palm in the hole that received the butt of the mast, raised sail again, and departed. The dying boy's cries for help smote his father's heart. Redechor dedicated himself to revenge. He had heard rumor of an island called Ngeredekus, inhabited by magicians, and he set sail there to seek help. As he neared the island, his sail disappeared. The magicians had been trolling when they saw the sail, had mistaken it for an approaching storm, and had used their magic to drive the rain away. Redechor paddled ashore. He told the magicians his story, and they agreed to help. They gave him magic ginger and instructions for its use. Redechor returned to Palau and stopped outside the Ngeruangel reef. Placing the magic ginger in the bow of his canoe, he pointed his stern toward Ngeruangel and he dug with a seashell deep into the sea. He brought the shell up brimming, held it toward Ngeruangel, and then dumped it upside down. Instantly a great hurricane arose and turned the atoll upside down. Redechor's destruction of Ngeruangel freed Kayangel, and Redechor is remembered as the savior of his atoll. Today redechor is the title of the dominant of Kayangel's two chiefs.

Later in its history, in the war between the United States and Japan, Ngeruangel was the scene of more conventional warfare, and today the remains of eight Japanese ships lie rusting on the circle of its reef, wreckage of a second empire. Ngeruangel is a shoal of ruined ambition.

JOHN KOCHI towed his boat toward Ngeruangel's lone island. His outboards were tilted out of the water. His baseball cap was turned visor forward, shading his eyes. He waded in the warm, shallow water of the island's lagoon side, leaning into the bowline like a Volga boatman, stepping slowly as he studied the birds on shore. The island was the last bit of territory in his domain, and as the conservation officer neared the beach, he was drawing to the end of Book One in his life. In a few days he would be leaving for the United States.

Kayangelese fishermen had built a cairn of coral stones as a point of elevation to warn them in high seas. The cairn rose from the sand like a vast and trunkless leg of stone. Otherwise the island was like bird islands everywhere. There was the burning beach, the birdlimed rocks, the blue desert of the sky, the sense of uninhabitableness. There was the seabird noise, like thousands of mechanical bird calls operated at random by small children. The bird noise all but drowned out the thud of surf on the island's ocean side. As each muted wave curled to break, a line of reflected suns exploded high along the glassy forward wall. The suns vanished in a smother of surf, to explode again as the next wave crested.

So on this island even the ocean, which should be cool, rebounded with light. There was no snag to cast a shadow, no outcrop for a fledgling tern to hide under. Most of the birds were white, and this absence of pigment seemed wrong in creatures that prospered in sand, that flew through air, so shot through with heat and brightness. Whiteness is a virtue in tropical birds, of course, but it took a moment to remember that. Kochi himself looked very dark under his baseball cap. Beneath his bare feet the bottom was sand and small chunks of coral. The chunks would have been very sharp to the soles of normal feet, but Kochi's did not feel them. Kochi's eyes, at the moment that normal eyesight first discerned the adult birds, had already made out the chicks running for the protection of their mothers. He had already laughed.

He was distracted from the birds by a four-foot shark in the shallow water ahead.

It is Kochi's belief that sharks come to Ngeruangel to catch birds. They are no danger to airborne birds, he says—nothing could be more obvious from above than a shark in two feet of water—but sometimes chicks fall or are driven into the lagoon, and the sharks wait for these. Kochi threw his bamboo pole like a spear. It looped through the air and hit the shark squarely in the head, fifty feet away. The shark planed off, its fin and tail slicing the surface.

Kochi retrieved his bamboo and continued shoreward. The water steadily became shallower and warmer. Seventy yards from shore it was just inches deep and hot enough to wash dishes in. Kochi walked more slowly. His every instinct told him to land and look around. He would have done so, but he knew that fear of man can drive chicks into the water. This very morning a Kayangelese woman had warned him of the danger. He was very pleased and proud that she had.

"There were only three (3) species of sea birds nesting in Ngeruangel reef," Kochi would report later, "the Crested terns, Gray-backed terns, and White terns. However, the Kayangel people has passed their conservation law protecting the area during the hatching period. That makes me unable to go to the birds. All I did was to go as close as possible, to about six or eight feet (6–8) from the land in order to make at least close to an affirmative identification range."

Kochi strained now at the leash of his bowline. He was so near the beach. He wanted to go ashore. He needed to go through with it. ("When I pick up a knife, I can't just fake it. I have to go through with it.") He wanted to land. Instead he wavered, like eelgrass leaning with the tide.

Then abruptly he turned on his heel. He had decided he was too close to the birds. He towed his boat into deeper water, aiming for the pass to the ocean. Soon the water was cool again around his toes, though hot still at the surface. He waded until he had enough depth for his outboards, and then a bit farther, just for the pleasure of the coolness around his chest. Then he climbed aboard, lowered his outboards, and yanked the starter cord. The boat raced over the clear green water of the reef's intermediate depths. Below, coral heads sped at the boat, distorted by the odd fishbowl effect where the bottom seems to be steeply and interminably rising in the direction the boat is traveling, yet never reaches top. Then suddenly the drop-off passed behind, and Singer was swinging out across the deep-blue swells of the open sea.

22

OWEN HELD a good-bye party for Kochi at the hotel. On the long banquet table there were mustard-colored napkins that matched the tablecloth, and long-stemmed wineglasses alongside the water tumblers. The hotel girls served steaks from New Zealand. It all seemed very strange for Palau. The entire staff of the biology lab was present, and everyone seemed a little embarrassed by the fine table and his own formal dress. At the end of the table Nina Dlutaoch was teaching one of the grounds keepers, Yaoch, how to use a fork. Yaoch's colleague Idesmang sat at the middle of the table with the two American guests on either side of him, isolated with no Palauan nearby to teach him about the fork. He waited, watching out of the corners of his eyes to see how it was done. Idesmang is a slow-talking, weathered, gentlemanly, resigned older man who likes his drink, but tonight he looked scrubbed and boyish. He sat very erect in his starched Hawaiian shirt. At last he began on his steak. Holding the fork between the wrong fingers, he bore down gingerly. He seemed worried that the fork would somehow catapult the steak off the table. He tried to get a feel for the fork's range of likely behavior.

At the head of the table Owen had his arm around Kochi and was giving last-minute advice. He was saying something about remembering goals, keeping one's eye on the goal. Something else about going around obstacles. Kochi awash in emotion, did not seem to be listening closely.

Owen tapped his water glass for silence. He rose and began a resonant and halting farewell speech. "We are here to wish John good-bye. For the benefit of Palau, and the entire Trust Territory, John is about to. . . ." When Owen finished, Kochi rose, eyes brimming, and promised not to let down his colleagues or the Trust Territory. The occasion now seemed a perversely American kind of torture—Ramona Kochi's eyes filled with tears as her husband spoke—but it did, in the end, let everyone know how they felt about everyone else.

THE NEXT MORNING, as he waited for the ferry to Babeldaob and the airfield, Kochi saw a big school of sardines in the channel. "Look at those fishes!" he said. "I wish I had my net!"

Later, as the climbing plane started its banking turn out to sea, Kochi nodded out the window in the direction of the reef. There was a white streak on the water.

"Outboard going out," he said.

PALAU'S INFLUENCE spreads outward from the archipelago like rings of water on a pond. The spreading circle overlaps circles from other archipelagos, and the interference pattern becomes complicated, but Palauanness is traceable for a surprising distance across the Pacific. Kochi was able to ride this diminishing ripple halfway to California. From Palau to Yap he conversed continuously with a Palauan friend about matters Palauan. At the Yap airfield there were Palauans he knew, and the Yapese quarantine officer had been a fellow student at the Trust Territory Farm Institute. At Guam airport there were expatriate Palauans, as well as Guamanians he had known in his high-school days. He spoke with these people as easily as if he last had seen them yesterday. In some cases he had, for Micronesian government officers travel continually in the Trust Territory, and several had been in Palau the day before. His Guamanian was not at all rusty, Kochi discovered.

Then he boarded a jet for Hawaii. This leg of his journey, the longest, was for Kochi like an astronaut's first weightless step. There were no Palauans around him in the cabin, only American faces. He began to lose assurance. He started to worry whether his entry papers were in order and whether it was proper to tuck his shirttails in or leave them out. When he landed at the Honolulu airport, he walked hurriedly to a phone booth to call nephews who were students in Hawaii. The number had seven digits, and Kochi asked for help in dialing. Palauan telephone numbers have only three. America was a seven-digit experience, and Kochi was not quite ready for it.

At the East-West Center, whose number he was calling to find his nephews, a Palauan happened to answer the phone, and Kochi happily broke into his native tongue. His confidence flowed back again. He got the address of his nephews, and in an hour he was sitting in their kitchen drinking coffee.

The nephews, Francisco and Moses Uludong, were students at the University of Hawaii. Kochi referred to them sometimes as nephews, sometimes as cousins. Palauan kinship is complicated by the Palauan custom of adopting everyone else's children. Palau's family trees make a jungle, and it takes a Palauan to understand them. The Uludong brothers were very happy to see their uncle, or whatever it was that Kochi was to them. Everybody sat around the kitchen table, beaming.

Francisco asked Kochi how long he was planning to attend school. "Four years," Kochi answered.

"Good, man. Good," Francisco said. "What field?" Kochi answered conservation, the brothers looked at each other and beamed even wider. "That's good, very good," said Moses. "We got to have strong conservation laws." Moses asked if Kochi was still crazy and hard-line in his enforcement of the conservation laws, arresting his brother and things like that. Sure, Kochi answered. He told them about bringing charges against the marine conservationist for taking undersized turtles. The story delighted the brothers.

The Uludongs wore Afros, or more accurately, Micros. Francisco, the older brother, wore a goatee. His face had an excited, scholarly incisiveness that was not quite Palauan. It seemed to be a face on the verge of decision. He watched Kochi unblinkingly across the kitchen table, and he seemed to see the older man for what he was. Francisco's eyes registered Kochi's boastfulness, wrinkling at the corners now and then, but his smile stayed appreciative. The strength and stubbornness of Kochi's stand on conservation was music to both Uludongs. There were too few older Palauans like that. Palau's history of foreign rule has made for figurehead chiefs and bootlicking native administrators, and there are no satisfactory Palauan heroes. It was lonely and fatiguing, Moses would later confess, for a young man to draw too much on himself as model. In speaking of a certain Palauan chief— "That crook! That shyster!"—Moses would admit that he admired the man. The chief was strong. He had strong beliefs. There was another Palauan chief, a better man, wiser and less selfish, a repository of Palauan tradition, but this chief went into a sort of soft-shoe for Americans, and even for Moses, who was just a student. That was not, said Moses, what he needed from the chief.

In Palau the Uludongs were famous revolutionaries. Two months earlier, when Moses was in Palau on vacation, he had been jailed for writing a death threat to a roving American ambassador. The death letter was anonymous, but the government knew that Moses and his brother were organizers of a radical student group called the Young Micronesians, and the government assumed that Moses was responsible—as he probably was. Moses angrily recalled the episode for Kochi. After his night in jail he went over to the hotel, where the ambassador was staying. There were two rows of policemen outside with rifles.

"Where's the big man?" Moses asked.

"Inside. You want to see him?"

"Yes," Moses answered. Then he stopped and stared at his countrymen. "You know, you look just like dummies to me, standing there. Don't you know that if I wanted to kill him, I would kill him?"

"We're just doing a job, Moses," said one of the policemen, smiling.

Moses was angry about his night in jail, but seeing his own people arrayed against him made him angrier. A policeman moved to block his path, but Moses stepped quickly around. He was beginning to find himself in the wild-eyed role that the populace had imagined for him. Inside, a police detective seated by the door pushed his chair away from the table, readying himself, when he saw Moses enter. Moses ignored the detective and strode to the table where the ambassador's party was eating. He had met the ambassador before and liked the man well enough, in a personal way. He put his arm around the ambassador's shoulder. He was too excited at the time to enjoy the Palauan insult in this overfamiliarity, but he enjoyed it later, in retrospect. He asked the ambassador how he was. The ambassador said something agreeable, but he would not look Uludong in the eyes.

"You know," said Moses, "you must be a very big man. You are the first American that just because he came here, a Palauan was put in jail. Look at me when I talk to you, man!" Then, unable to control a sudden fury, Moses had turned and walked from the room, cursing in Palauan.

At their kitchen table the Uludongs seemed, in spite of their reputation, to be gentle young men. Their revolutionary convictions were hardening, and they were confronting the problem of violence, unable to resolve it. When the conversation at the kitchen table turned to one American who works in Palau for the Trust Territory government, Francisco spoke angrily. "Palauans hate that man," he said. "He's been there ten years, and he hasn't done anything. Not a thing. Goddamn, I hate that guy." When Moses suggested that, because of the American's connections at headquarters in Saipan and at the Interior Department, he was probably unoustable, Francisco said, "Then maybe we should shoot him." He was not simply practicing his rhetoric; there was too much real toughness in his words. Clearly it was a question he had been asking himself lately. "Maybe we should shoot him?"

The Uludong's older sister Anna Marie arrived, baby on arm. She was a sturdy, pretty Palauan expatriate in her thirties, with love-pledge burn welts on her strong upper arm and her black hair tied in braids. She was married to a native Hawaiian and lived on the windward side of the island. She was very happy to see Kochi.

"You look terrible!" she said to her brothers. "You want me to cut your hair? Are you so poor you can't get a haircut?" The Uludongs smiled. They were used to this harassment. "If I cut my hair, I would lose all my girl friends," Francisco said.

Kochi remembered with a start that he had betel nut, and he announced it to the room. Francisco and Moses were happy but incredulous, for few Micronesians they knew had been able to get betel nut through the agricultural inspection. Kochi produced the betel-nut bag, woven of pandanus, and passed it around. In no time everyone was happily seated on the floor, with cheeks big, teeth red, and the air full of the green fragrance of chewed betel nut and kebui leaf. Joe Keola, Anna Marie's husband, did not chew, but he was happy watching his Palauan in-laws enjoy themselves. Anna Marie's cheek was to be big all day. She never stopped chewing.

"You should be more careful," she said to her revolutionary brothers, starting in on them again. "You should stop all this nonsense. Why do you worry so much for others? Why don't you worry about yourselves?"

Moses smiled and groaned simultaneously at the baldness of that. "That's what all Palauans say. 'Why do you fight for Palau? Fight for yourself.' That's why Palau can't get anyplace today."

ANNA MARIE decided that Kochi would spend the night at her house and catch a flight to California in the morning. Everyone but Francisco, who had business elsewhere, piled into Joe Keola's car for the trip home.

As Keola drove through Honolulu, Moses and Kochi talked. Moses told Kochi that if a chief, ibedul or reklai, had told him to shut up about the American ambassador, to forget about it, he would have done so immediately. But no one had spoken to him but the district administrator, Tom Remengesau, a man appointed by the Americans. Then Moses spoke of Koror Town. "They have one hour of Palauan songs out of fourteen hours of radio, and they call it Radio Palau! The street signs are all in English. In the nightclubs the people dance to American music, and they wouldn't begin to know how to dance Palauan. And me! I learned American ways before Palauan! If you asked me how many clans there were, and what districts they came from—you know, even just the big clans—I couldn't tell you."

Keola stopped the car at a big Honolulu fish market and everyone went in to shop. The market excited Kochi, who recognized familiar fish among the many kinds for sale. He walked along the counter, pointing through the glass at big-eyed squirrelfish, milkfish, unicornfish, and naming them aloud. The fish were threads in the fabric of his old life, but it was a fabric that was already getting strange on him. Many of the fish were unfamiliar, and those he knew were labeled with Hawaiian names like *awa* and *u-u*. It sounded like baby talk after the more stately Palauan.

After leaving the fish market, Joe Keola, who was a computer repairman, stopped at his job to show Kochi and Moses the computers. It might have seemed a rash move, an unnecessarily abrupt step in Kochi's transition to civilization. At five the previous morning Kochi had taken his son Stevie into the cassava patch for a last grave conversation, and at seven he had been gazing at a school of sardines in the Babeldaob channel, itching for his casting net. But the computers did not seem to impress Kochi much, one way or the other.

Keola loved the computers, clearly. He walked around the room describing the capabilities of the different machines. He stopped by one that could print 1,100 lines of 132 characters per minute. He tapped out a brief instruction on the keyboard, and the computer typed dozens of lines of the numeral 1. Moses shook his head. "The Machine Age!" he said. "It's coming, man. We're already in it!"

Joe Keola had not said much in the car earlier. He had been listening to his brother-in-law's political conversation, clearly, for he now typed out a new program, the words "freedom for micronesia" followed by the program code.

"Error in syntax," the International Business Machine answered, and it refused to repeat the message.

They left the computers and drove on to the Keola house. Joe and Anna Marie were doing very well, from the look of things. There was a workshop for Joe, a pool table, a big aquarium full of tropical fish. When Anna Marie got home she put the betel nut in the crisper of her big refrigerator. She showed Kochi the dry taro she was growing in her backyard. She seemed worried about the taro, and she asked Kochi how the plants looked to him.

"Hey! TV has color film already!" said Kochi when he turned on the television that night.

THE NEXT MORNING the Uludongs drove Kochi to the airport, and he resumed his journey.

There was now no longer anything recognizable beneath his plane window. The very texture of the globe had been changing since he left Palau. The chaotic cloud cover of the Carolines—clouds at all altitudes and of all sizes and shapes—in Hawaii had simplified to great domes of cumulus over those mountainous islands. Now, after Hawaii, the clouds thinned, lengthened, and lay in endless windrows on the ocean. Then the windrows themselves thinned, and disappeared, and the ocean was naked below. For a long time the desert of the North Pacific passed beneath. It seemed a colder ocean. And then they were losing altitude, or appeared to be, for whitecaps were now visible. And then, at dusk, without warning after all those blue leagues of ocean, came the coast of California. The march of the waves simply ended against it. The coast was long and straight and stretched as far as the eye could see. It was a wild part of the coast, and few lights were burning.

In the San Francisco airport, deplaning among American men, Kochi did not look so large. He wore his old army low-quarters, the only shoes he owned, and a short-sleeved shirt that was too thin for the weather. He carried a small twenty-pound suitcase. There was no warmer clothing inside the suitcase, just Kochi's conservation books, his baseball glove, his face mask, and his fins.

When I am able, I drive up to Eureka, California, to see how Kochi is doing in school. I follow the Redwood Highway, named for the great trees that once covered the northern California coast. It's a country of small roads and big logging trucks. The trucks come fast, pulling vacuums behind them through the narrow corridors of remnant big trees, buffeting you in the other lane. Pieces of fibrous red bark from the trucks lie on the road, like unidentifiable flattened animals. Redwoods are fog-forest trees, and the steep wooded hills are often ragged with mist.

Eureka is on the ocean, a happy choice by those who planned Kochi's coming. The Pacific here has an arctic chill, however. The skies above Eureka are overcast more often than Palau's, and the storms take longer to blow over. When summer storms have passed, the day is bright-cool instead of bright-humid. Eureka, a dying logging town, is a small community, another good choice for Kochi, the small-islander. The air is clean, frequently washed by rain, Kochi's room is small and sparsely furnished, like his house in Palau. But in the tropics a simplicity of interiors is somehow hospitable; here in the Pacific Northwest it seems bleak.

Kochi is glad to see me, because I remind him of Palau. We exchange news of the islands. There is plenty of news. Desire for independence and dislike of Americans is growing in Micronesia. Recently a big turtle spear flew militantly through the screen of Robert Owen's bungalow, passing between Owen and the man he was talking to. Owen sometimes thinks of leaving, but continues to stay on.

One time I gave Kochi the news, a little too abruptly, that Ibedul Ngeriakl had died. Kochi was visibly shaken. I was surprised, for Kochi had never been one of those in awe of ibedul. Then Kochi explained how important high chief ibedul was to the well-being of the Palauan people, whatever you thought of the man who held the title. Kochi began to worry, here in California, thousands of miles away, about who would be ibedul's successor.

Kochi hangs on. He continues to get passing grades. He misses Palau and is sometimes lonely. There is no proper tragedy in any of this, I suppose, yet the trips to the redwood country make me uneasy. Kochi in California is not quite himself. For me, he is colorless on the continent. Like one of the prismatic fish he used to unhook and toss to the floor of his boat, Kochi's true shades began to ebb the instant he left his own waters. I have no reason to believe that the loss is permanent. I hope, and believe, that Kochi's color will return the moment he is tossed back into his context.

Kenneth Brower was born in San Francisco in 1944. The son of David Brower, a seminal leader of the conservation movement and currently president of Friends of the Earth, his earliest memories are of the wilderness of the American West. He has edited seven exhibit format volumes, among them: *Kauai and the Park Country of Hawaii, Baja California and the Geography of Hope, Navajo Wildland: As Long as the Rivers Shall Run,* and *Galapagos: The Flow of Wildness,* of which he was co-author. He has assembled three volumes in the Earth's Wild Places series under the auspices of Friends of the Earth: *Maui: The Last Hawaiian Place; Earth and Ocean: the Primal Alliance;* and *Earth and the Great Weather: The Brooks Range.* His work has taken him to Alaska, the Galapagos, the Hawaiian Islands, and Micronesia.